The Regional Books Series

GENERAL EDITOR: BRIAN VESEY-FITZGERALD, F.L.S.

PEMBROKESHIRE

THE REGIONAL BOOKS SERIES

Edited by Brian Vesey-FitzGerald, F.L.S.

THE Regional Books *deal in the fullest manner with certain highly individual and remarkable areas of Britain. In every instance the Region itself is a clear-cut entity, with a marked individuality of its own.*

The following volumes have been published.

PEMBROKESHIRE

R. M. LOCKLEY

SECOND EDITION

ROBERT HALE & COMPANY
63 Old Brompton Road, London S.W.7

By the same Author

DREAM ISLAND DAYS

THE ISLAND DWELLERS

I KNOW AN ISLAND

THE WAY TO AN ISLAND

THE SEA'S A THIEF

SHEARWATERS

A POT OF SMOKE

EARLY MORNING ISLAND

INLAND FARM

BIRDS OF THE SEA

ISLANDS ROUND BRITAIN

THE ISLAND FARMERS

LETTERS FROM SKOKHOLM

THE GOLDEN YEAR

THE CHARM OF THE CHANNEL ISLANDS

THE NATURE-LOVERS' ANTHOLOGY

GILBERT WHITE: A BIOGRAPHY

TRAVELS WITH A TENT IN WESTERN EUROPE

PUFFINS

THE SEALS AND THE CURRAGH

IN PRAISE OF ISLANDS

SEA-BIRDS (WITH JAMES FISHER)

ISLAND OF SKOMER (WITH JOHN BUXTON)

In collaboration with Dr. Julian Huxley, the film:
' The Private Life of the Gannets'

SBN 7091 0781 1

© R. M. Lockley 1957, 1965 and 1969

First published February 1957
Reprinted May 1958
Reprinted August 1961
New edition July 1965
New edition February 1969

PRINTED IN GREAT BRITAIN BY
LOWE AND BRYDONE (PRINTERS) LIMITED, LONDON, N.W.10

CONTENTS

ILLUSTRATIONS

vii

ILLUSTRATIONS

A sketch-map is included at the end of the book but for more detailed information readers are referred to the respective Ordnance Survey sheets.

ACKNOWLEDGMENTS

The illustrations nos. 16, 18, 19 and 21 are reproduced from photographs supplied by S. H. Clarke; nos. 3, 4 and 14 by Miss M. Wight; nos. 1, 5 and 20 by Frank Rogers; nos. 6 and 9 by A. W. Nineham; the remaining 13 photographs were supplied by the author.

viii

FOREWORD

"Soe this litle Countie of Pembroksheere is not without plentie of Gods blessing as well for sufficient meanes for the people to live in good and plentifull sort."

GEORGE OWEN, 1603

THUS wrote her loving and loyal historian; and from the first to the second Elizabethan age, Pembrokeshire has remained one of the least changed of the counties of England and Wales. Her population, in relation to the national increase, has even declined, and is still that of a moderate provincial town—under one hundred thousand. For this there are many reasons which will appear in due course in this account of the most westerly county of Wales. George Owen described Pembrokeshire as "neyther perfect square longe nor round but shaped with diverse Corners, some sharpe, some obtuse, in some places concave in some convexe, but in most places concave and bendinge inwarde, as doth the Moone in her decreaseinge"; where "the westerlye and south windes are founde very sharpe and tempestuouse, soe the Countrey for the most parte beinge champion [plain] and open, the trees appear bendinge and shorne with those windes, soe that a straunger maye travell knoweinge in what eate [direction] of the winde his jorney lyeth by the bendinge of the trees, as the Mariner dothe by his compasse at sea". Which is very true.

Owen liked to quote the famous historian, Giraldus Cambrensis (Gerald the Welshman), who was born in 1147 at Manorbier Castle in the south of the county. For Gerald, in all his itineraries and wanderings, had found no fairer land than Pembrokeshire; over it he believed blew twice purified air—air originating, in the first place, from Ireland (a country he knew to be exceptionally healthy because no venomous creatures lived there) and, secondly, further sweetened by Atlantic ozone.

Gerald and his admirer Owen were stout champions of Pembrokeshire, in which their ancestral roots were deep. They were men who fulfilled the saying that he who has regard for his ancestors will have regard for his posterity. Both men claimed descent from the Welsh prince Rhys ap Tewdwr, a famous figure in the history of Wales. Gerald's grandmother was Rhys's daughter Nesta, a most beautiful woman after whom to this day many a plainer Welshwoman has been christened. Nesta, known in popular history as the Helen of Wales, married Gerald de Windsor, castellan of the Norman stronghold of Pembroke, but she was also mistress of Henry II.

George Owen was born at Henllys in 1552 and lived in this mountainous north half of the county, among the indigenous Welsh. Every chapter of his *Description of Penbrockshire* (1603) breathes a militant affection for the county.

A third historian was Richard Fenton, gentleman, born in 1747 at St David's in the north-west of the county; he too claimed descent or connection by marriage with the princely line of Giraldus. He wrote *A Historical Tour through Pembrokeshire* (1811), an engaging account which modern historians rather despair of because of its inaccuracies, some of which are the natural consequence of later discoveries: but antiquarians have not forgiven Fenton his rather light-hearted and unscientific excavations of tumuli and ancient graves. He was a friend of Oliver Goldsmith. After a semi-literary career in London he retired to Fishguard, where he reorganised the shipping business left to him by his uncle, and had the leisure at the same time to indulge his love of scribbling historical communications.

Many names, some of persons living today, doubtless qualify for the position of fourth historian, but I would choose the late Edward Laws for his *History of Little England Beyond Wales & the Non-Kymric Colony Settled in Pembrokeshire* (1888), in which enthusiasm and humour are blended with scientific perspicacity and a vast energy. He was a scholar, antiquarian and honorary secretary of the Cymrodorian Society, and lived much in Tenby. His preamble to his book ends with the words: "If my reader admits that it is worth while to *try* and write the history of Little England beyond Wales then I claim that my Preamble is proven." He certainly tried—the book is nearly 500 large quarto pages.

This is as fair and appropriate a mixture of county historians to draw upon as the modern historiographer could wish: two from the north and two from the south. For Pembrokeshire is remarkable for the very clear division of its history and topography into two natural halves. In the north is a Welsh-speaking pastoral people inhabiting the hills and mountains; in the south a people speaking exclusively English, living on a rich cultivated plain. These halves are sometimes known respectively as the *Welshery* and the *Englishery*. The Englishery is the true "Little England beyond Wales", the *Anglia Transwalliana* of Camden. Dividing the two is a sharp geographical and ethnological demarcation line known as the *Landsker*, a word derived from old Viking associations. The Landsker follows roughly the line of castles from west to east through the centre of the county, from Roch castle on the west coast, through Haverfordwest, Picton, Wiston, Lawhaden, and Narberth castles to Amroth castle; these defended the southern half of the county from the stubborn Welsh whom the Normans had dispossessed, and behind this frontier are other castles, defending the south in depth.

South of the Landsker the county is a plateau, about 200 feet above sea-level, of rich farm land on limestone and old red sandstone, split by the grand fiord of Milford Haven, which provided the easiest access for the export and import trade in the days before rail and road transport killed the profit on cargoes carried coastwise in sailing ships.

North of the Landsker the county grows poorer agriculturally as it becomes richer scenically. In these hills and mountains dwells the true Welsh-speaking peasant stock, hardy, capable of thriving where an Englishman would starve, tenacious of a heritage probably little disturbed since man arrived after the ice last retreated from Wales. The builders of the dolmens lived here: megalithic cromlechs and stone circles and burial mounds abound more than in any other place in Britain. The blue stones of the inner ring of Stonehenge came from north Pembrokeshire. Into this wild sanctuary retreated the native people after each invasion by foreigners, of which there were many—Neolithic, Roman, Irish, Saxon, Scandinavian, Norman, Fleming and English—who coveted the smiling tableland of the south, but who could make little headway through the hills and bogs of the north.

These waves have left their tide-marks, as jetsam of the sea lies upon a beach, in place-names and in the appearance and speech of the people themselves.

As for my qualifications to write this book, I am a piece of Pembrokeshire jetsam myself. My grandfather was Captain David Mathias, of Flemish extraction, who married Jane Williams, daughter of a Welsh priest. He sailed a barque on the "tea and teak" East Indies route. My father was an Englishman of Scotch extraction from the Welsh border: but my mother was born at Milford Haven, and in Pembrokeshire I have lived for most of my life. For thirteen years I lived on the Pembrokeshire island of Skokholm, then for nine years on the north coast, and for the next ten years in the south of the county. I have travelled every road and lane and footpath in the county, farmed over 1,000 of her acres, and sailed in and out of every bay of the whole coast. It was my privilege and pleasure to walk the coast and map out for the National Parks Commission the present footpath of the lately established Pembrokeshire Coast National Park. This book is specially written for the people who come to see Pembrokeshire today, often because of its designation as a National Park. But it is written for all who would and do know and like the county, too.

This book is written at Orielton, near Pembroke, a great house re-built in 1656, but its foundations date at least from the days when it was a fortified manor owned by Norman knights of the twelfth century. Its high red sandstone walls enclose 260 acres of wood, water and farmland, and make a perfect natural sanctuary.

I am indebted to many people for assistance, which I have tried to acknowledge within these pages, in preparing this book. To all of them I offer my warmest thanks.

R. M. L.

CHAPTER I

EARLY HISTORY

SUCH were the tales my mother told of her father's sea-journeys that I could picture his tall ship full of sail gliding up the wide haven of Milford, or plunging under bare poles around the Cape of Good Hope. I would stare at the portrait in oils of this fair, bearded man which hung in the drawing-room of our house; then I would look at the water-colour, six inches square, of the barque rip-snorting along a lonely yellow coast.

Was he the valorous romantic figure I pictured Captain David Mathias to be? Vaguely I remember now the answers I got to my questions about the mixed cargoes he shipped to the east: apparently toys and trinkets, and tea and teak homewards. His wife bore him three daughters and a son; the son went to sea as a mid-shipman and was drowned. After that the still young captain brought his last cargo home to Milford and set up as a timber merchant with his wife's brother, another sea-captain. But somehow the business did not flourish. The mid-Victorian boom was over. Also David Mathias on land was as miserable as an albatross tied by one leg ashore. He spent much of his time staring out to sea with a telescope, identifying the sailing ships which came to anchor opposite the south-sloping terraces of the new town of Milford Haven. He died before I was born, leaving nothing but this aura of salt romance on which his daughter fed his grandson to such an extent that I ever longed to see the environment in which my mother had so graphically pictured grandfather—the great red-walled fiord of Milford Haven.

My grandfather had been named after the patron saint of Wales. And to St David's I went for my second taste of the rich heady air of Pembrokeshire. My first had been to Amroth on the south-east frontier of the county, at the age of ten.

The lethargic bus from Haverfordwest chugged sixteen miles over seventeen hills to reach the treeless village-city, and from

I   I

thence three callow youths of sixteen carried their packs down to the uninhabited sea-glen of Caerbwdy. Here stood a cabin washed ashore straight from the deck of a small ship: we adopted it, cleaning and painting it out. The loveliness of that furze-beyellowed bay made me determine then that my life should be lived in Pembrokeshire. The three boys camping alone discovered untarnished nature in the best way possible, by running wild and free in pursuit of her wonders, losing the soft shell of suburban civilisation in carefree adventures by sea and shore.

We lived much on the produce of rod, line, gun and snare: rabbits, eels in the stream, pollack and mackerel in the sea. We flung the scraps of our fish and coney meals upon a high rock near the camp and watched the buzzard hawks spiral down from the clouds to devour this carrion. Along the coast were small flocks of the rare chough or red-billed crow. There were peregrine falcons diving upon jackdaws and rock-doves. Sea-birds and sea-ducks trailed in echelon off shore. Seals swam in surf below, as we walked along the high headlands facing the twin hills and white tide-races of Ramsey Island.

Far in the south, across the wide bay of St Bride's, lay other islands with Norse names: Skomer, Skokholm, and away to the south-west the lonely islet of Grassholm; and beyond was the far fingerpost of the Smalls lighthouse. I dreamed, without great hope, that one day I would live on one of those islands.

For the present we were happy enough, living in large capitals beyond our narrow experience. Everything was grand and beautiful and remarkable and awe-inspiring—the gigantic clear blue sea with its majestic billows bearing the heady moist Atlantic winds, the brilliant new flowers and new birds of the shore; and by night the great starry cupola of heaven without a man-made sign to indicate civilisation within our horizon, unless it was a far lighthouse flashing in the empty westward ocean.

Every step by Dyfed's pure sea was upon soil and rock consecrated by unknown centuries of treading by ancient man. In the purple cliffs of Caerbwdy was a great scar where the stone had been taken to rebuild the Cathedral of St David after one of its sackings by sea-pirates. In the cathedral itself was a casket said to contain the bones of the saint himself, the man who did so much to bring Christianity into the lives of the Celts which were then dominated by the blood-sacrifices of the ceremonies of the Druids.

St David was the last prophet, and Christianity the latest religion, to assume power here over the minds of the people; but everywhere was evidence of a religion thousands of years older in the stone circles, cromlechs and cliff dwellings of men who like ourselves had worshipped the sun and the stars and Nature. When we wandered over St David's Head and hunted for birds and flowers I seemed to see the long heads of Silurian men, women and children peeping from the lichen-crowned rocks. In their hands were rough stone axes and slings—and perhaps a hairy mammoth strolled in the distance. . . .

Who were these builders in stone? How did they come here, and how did they live? Who went before them? And who before that? Hadn't I learned it all vaguely before—in school? But somehow, locked up in classrooms, I had found history indigestible— much of it had been read to us, I remembered, by a master who loved to recite from his own books! Here, in the open, this history seemed but yesterday, and I was burning to know the answers.

As it turned out we had been exploring over primitive rocks which, excepting certain formations in North America, are believed to be the oldest in the world. Pembrokeshire for millions of years may have been a rocky height standing above the sludge of primeval seas. Some of the earliest forms of life appear in the giant fossil tribolites or wood-louse-like crustaceans in the pre-Cambrian beds at St David's, which may be 500 million years old. Earth movements folded and heaved these rocks into view, weather denuded their overlying sediments, and the ice-sheets sheared away much. The northern half of the county shows many of these ancient igneous formations, between beds of shale; but the southern half is geologically newer—old red sandstone, and carboniferous limestone containing fish and the shells of sea-animals.

The reptilian ancestors of the first land animals lived in the triassic period over 150 million years ago; 100 million years later they dominated the scene, but have ever since been declining. As far as this book is concerned there is only space to consider the last million years. During that period there were at least four glaciations of between 50 thousand and 100 thousand years, with longer interglacial warm periods, of which the present one has so far only lasted some 20 thousand years. Between these inter-glaciated periods Pleistocene man appeared in the British Isles, associated with the descendants of the dinosaurs—the mammoth, rhinoceros, hippopotamus, tiger, lion, hyena, elk, reindeer, musk-ox, wild horse, and other mammals, some now extinct, whose remains have been found numerously in caves in the lime-stone of south Pembrokeshire.

These animals roamed the great plain of what is now the Bristol Channel, which may have extended out to the present 100-fathom line of the Continental Shelf, beyond Ireland. Britain was then undivided from Europe; the animals could retreat southwards at the advance of each Ice Age, and move north again into this land when the ice melted. Unaccommodating forms such as the elephant-like mastodons and the sabre-toothed tigers died out first, and various species of mammoths and lions suc-ceeded. In warm periods hippopotami moved up into British rivers and swamps, and when the glaciers returned there were musk-ox and reindeer living in Britain. Of all these animals pre-historic man took toll; he slew them with his primitive tools, trapped them, or ate them when they had died. He brought their bones into the caves where he lived.

These prehistoric bones in the limestone caves in the south-east of Pembrokeshire have been beautifully preserved by the action of carbonate of lime. Caves at Caldey Island, at Hoyle's Mouth and Little Hoyle near Tenby, and the Black Rock Quarry (at Coygan just over the border near Laugharne) have yielded a rich store of animal bones: the collection covers the mammoth, woolly rhinoceros, hippopotamus, brown and cave bears, wolf, fox, hyena, lion, Irish elk, red deer, reindeer, wild ox, bison, horse, as well as the first domestic animals—goat, pig and dog.

These caves were the lairs, larders, dens and last resting-places of the earliest Man of Knowing, *homo sapiens*. Between him and the hominids or ape-like men of half a million years earlier there is as yet no very obvious missing link found (the Piltdown skull is proved after all a fake) before the sea last billowed over the lands of the Bristol Channel. These were the legendary Lost Lands of Lyonesse of the west which historians laughed at but which nevertheless the prehistorians have now proved to have existed, rich with the giant animals, plants and men which this world will never see living again.

When exactly the Acheulean men who were living in Britain a quarter of a million years ago left is not known, but in some glaciated period they vanished. It is interesting to learn (now that the Piltdown man has been discredited) that he was little different in appearance from modern man, with a large brain and with better bone and teeth. His implements of flint were more finely shaped as cutting tools than those of the first men, the Chelleans and their ancestors.

Next came Neanderthal man, contemporary with woolly rhinoceros, mammoth, reindeer, musk-ox, cave-bear and wild oxen. He was extinct about 70,000 B.C. The last glaciers retreated from Britain some 50,000 years later; with their melting the shores of western Europe subsided, and about 6500 B.C. the sea finally enisled Britain. Ireland was probably separated somewhat earlier.

Flint is no longer found naturally in Pembrokeshire but nevertheless thousands of flints have been discovered in or near the caves on Caldey, which must therefore date from before the inundation; they are of both old and new (Neolithic) stone age and were doubtless carried down by the north ice; these and other Pembrokeshire limestone caves show traces of occupation by man right down to Romano-British times.

Neolithic man made wooden handles for his polished flint weapons; he cultivated the soil and grew wheat, oats, barley and rye. He was a potter, weaved cloth from his sheep, made ropes of hair, but had no knowledge of metals. How he reached Britain is a matter of conjecture, but he was of that race which subsequently built mighty monuments of unhewn stone. He lived on into the centuries when the pyramids were erected in Egypt; it is supposed that the cromlech-builders originated in the eastern Mediterranean. They were dark-haired and long-headed. They were competent mariners. Their chambered tombs can be traced across the Mediterranean westwards through Sardinia, the Iberian coast, Brittany, the Channel Islands, Cornwall, Wales, Ireland and south-west Scotland. These are nowhere in Britain more plentiful than in north Pembrokeshire. The date of their erection is usually fixed at about 2000 B.C.

These colonists from the Mediterranean, sailing their boats on the fringe of the wild Atlantic, may have been young men who collected wives from among the more primitive settled peoples they encountered on their voyages. It has been shown that builders of megaliths and the earlier Mesolithic folk lived together in northern Ireland. The erection of the great stone tomb in its various forms probably gave the newcomers a superior status, that of an awe-inspiring priesthood; we know that rites were practised at these places associated with fertility, as well as with the transference of a benign spirit to newcomers (including the new-born) to the community. The stone passage or gallery grave may well have been the site of a burial ceremony in which the deceased (or his head perhaps only) was carried in at one end; later, possibly after a considerable interval, the priest would visit the remains and declare the spirit ready to be freed, and he would emerge at the other end of the grave. Then would follow a ceremonial dance or performance which welcomed the spirit of the departed back to earth again, perhaps in the form of a white stone—a frequent object in many such graves. Its presence in the chambered tomb represented the vital essence of life, for the Neolithic tribe.

There are in Pembrokeshire twenty-six cromlechau or burial chambers (having three or more standing stones supporting a capstone), twenty standing stones (*meini hirion*) of tribal significance, twenty-seven round burial barrows or earth or stone memorial cairns, and about seventy earthworks, hill forts or camps of later (Early Iron) age.

Most remarkable fact and feat, indisputably proved by the geologist H. H. Thomas in 1923, was the transfer of over thirty huge sacred stones from Pembrokeshire (150 miles as the crow flies) to Stonehenge on Salisbury Plain, between 1600 and 1400

B.C., proving that what we now know as Pembrokeshire was a region of special importance at that time. The construction of Stonehenge shows that the architectural skill and organisation of labour of the megalithic man was at its height. Its erection may have followed perhaps the arrival of new fanatical priests of the cult from Pembrokeshire. Salisbury Plain was evidently the north-western vatican of the late Stone Age culture, and here probably priests and the common people gathered to receive the archpriest's blessing and witness the ceremonies.

How these heavy stones were moved is not proved, but the simplest hypothesis is that they were transhipped by sea. The four heavy rhyolite and twenty-nine dolerite blocks came from the cairns (*Alw* and *Meini*) on the shoulder of the Prescelly mountains; these could have been dragged on rollers or sledges to the sea at Newport, Pem., or to the river Cleddau, and taken thence by sea to the river Avon in Hampshire; or, as has also been suggested, up the Severn and along the Mendip hills to the Plain. The more arduous way, entirely by land, involving the crossing of rivers, seems most unlikely. The priests and engineers in charge of the operation must have had plenty of man-power in the form of slaves or fanatical followers. The so-called sacred centre or altar stone of Stonehenge, of fine-grained micaceous sandstone, comes from Cosheston, which lies conveniently for loading beside the upper tide-waters of Milford Haven; upon this stone the beams of the rising sun touched at the summer solstice, passing through the mouth of the double horseshoe of local sarsen and Pembrokeshire stones which lay open to the north-east. The archaeological and astronomical data support the popular theory that Stonehenge was a temple of the sun-god, the giver of warmth and life, as well as a sundial for recording seasons and solstices.

A series of 500 photographs of the upright stones recently taken from different angles and heights has revealed incised drawings, of daggers and axes. These carvings represent full-size specimens of the Irish flanged axe, comparable with the Minoan cult of the Double Axe. Nothing like these has been found previously in north-western Europe, and it is therefore possible that these carvings were executed at Stonehenge in the lifetime of a sculptor familiar with this type of weapon in Greece, that is to say about 1475 B.C. If so, this gives a firmer date to Stonehenge, within the Bronze Age.

It is common to read of the overthrow of the Neolithic, long-headed stone builders by the round-headed so-called Beaker people who migrated from the east, from Holland and the Rhine. These newcomers were an Aryan riverine people who carried metal weapons, chiefly of bronze, in their hands and who placed vases or stone beakers in their graves. Later research and discovery suggest that the transition must have been very gradual, that the first beaker people may have not brought metal; there was inter-marriage, and the round-heads mingled with the long-heads in the ceremonies to the sun-god on Salisbury Plain, around which, as in Pembrokeshire, the long barrows of the long-heads and the round barrows of the round-heads both appear, apparently contemporaneously. To this day it is said one may see in remote valleys in Wales a dark-eyed long-headed race. These people have been found to belong to the same blood-group with other dark long-heads persisting in hardy remote peasant communities in the British Isles. I have seen this type commonly in the Prescelly mountains and the neighbouring valleys of Carmarthenshire, where marriage between cousins is not infrequent, fixing these characters as inbreeding will do. The Romans found the type still dominating much of western Wales.

The Bronze Age round-barrow round-heads cremated their dead, and placed them in cinerary urns, whereas the old-fashioned long-heads buried them. But occasionally something went wrong or the fashion changed, and we find long-head skeletons in round barrows, or round-heads buried, not burnt, there. In these round tumps, so plentiful in south Pembrokeshire, are found bronze weapons and tools, some deliberately broken in order to "kill" them, so that their ghosts could accompany the ghost of their owner on his journey into the unknown. On top of the mounds the remains of the funeral feast are the first objects encountered by the excavator or desecrator: bones of horse, ox, sheep, goat, pig, deer, dog, and near the coast, shellfish. Laws notes that he never opened a Pembrokeshire tump without finding white pebbles; these are associated, as we have seen, with neolithic burial ceremonies.

The burial mounds, whether round or chambered, evidently had a special effect on local residents. Here dwelt the spirits of the dead, who were all powerful to protect those who raised the mounds and their descendants, so that enemies were less inclined to risk the evil influence upon them which would follow any attempt to violate rights or territory (hunting grounds and farms) belonging to the ancestral spirits.

The exclusive use of bronze lasted long in the west and continued probably centuries after the discovery of the use of iron and until about 500 B.C. But before the coming of the Romans there was a dark obscure period in Welsh history, coinciding with a period of rainy Atlantic weather. The botanical evidence surviving from that time in peat and other deposits indicates a cold wet spell in which lakes rose and flooded settlements and people were forced to live on hills and along the seashore. Culture suffered in the effort to survive the damp, wet, depressing conditions.

Meanwhile at this period the lake-dwellers at La Tène on Neuchatel (Switzerland) appeared to have been the prolific centre of a Celtic-speaking culture which sent forth colonists in all westerly directions, having originated, it is thought, on the Russian steppes. By the time this culture reached Wales it had assumed the form known as Druidism, and brought a language which, no doubt modified by the mixed tongue of the ancient longhead and beaker peoples, has resulted in the Welsh we know today.

Druidism was a religion of reincarnation, and incorporated the bloody practice of disembowelling human victims. According to Strabo (III, c. 6) the Iberian Celts "divined by the entrails of captive enemies, and when (these are) stricken by the soothsayer, draw their first augury from the fall of the entrails". Tacitus reports the drenching of altars with human blood by the Welsh druids. Suetonius Paulinus made his legionaries in Anglesey cut down the sacred groves of the cult, although perhaps less out of disgust for their practices (since the Romans were notorious for sacrificing human life) than because he feared the power and enmity of this powerful sect.

Druidism still flourished in Pembrokeshire at the time of the appearance of the Welsh-born men who became saints, Patrick and David. At this time, when the Roman influence, which hardly touched Pembrokeshire, was waning in Britain, the Irish Christians were spreading their culture back towards the east. About A.D. 250–300 some of the men of the Deisi tribes from Ireland appear to have settled in Pembrokeshire, and began that process of spreading the gospel which reached its most fervent stage during the lives of Patrick and David.

St Patrick seems to have been born about the year A.D. 373 in "Vallis Rosina" at St David's. His mother Conchessa was said to be sister to St Martin, Bishop of Tours, who instructed his nephew as a young priest so successfully that he became famous in, and after his death the patron saint of, Ireland. He had been carried off as a young man to Ireland, the captive of Irish pirates raiding Pembrokeshire.

It was while St Patrick was preaching one day at St David's as an old man of about eighty-seven, that his eye lighted upon Nonnita, then pregnant with the unborn David, and for a while he became dumb with a heavenly vision. It is recorded that he received the premonition that Nonnita was carrying the future saint who would complete the work of christianising Wales which he had begun.

Many other legends are told of St David. Historians are apt to say that his recorded Life is largely spurious. He was born about the year 462, grandson, we are told, of the Welsh nobleman Ceredigion (Cardigan), whose son Sandde violated a nun. Nonnita is said to have given birth to David at or near the windswept site of Non's Well, which is on the coast south of St David's. Of his early life we have few records. He was educated at Whitland Abbey for the priesthood. He finally settled in the Vallis Rosina, the little glen where lay the monastic settlement, characteristic of the early Celtic churches, begun by St Patrick.

St David may have been no less remarkable than later accounts pretend: but down to medieval times his fame had won him no

dedication north of south Wales. The north Wales saints came
from another direction—the north: Saints Beuno, Kentigern,
Tysylio, and the descendants of Coel Godebog, Cunedda,
etc. Nevertheless there are several ancient dedications to St
David southwards, in Devon and Cornwall and Brittany,
although one cannot be sure they are all to the same David, the
Welshman known to Welshmen as Dewi Sant. At that time
Welsh (Brythonic) was the common language of Wales, Cornwall and Brittany (a Welshman today can still converse with a
Breton, although there are marked dialectic differences). There
was a freely used seaway between the three, and evidently
plenty of disciples ready to establish the cult of St David southwards in these Celtic communities, even if the saint himself
did not travel there in the flesh.

St David was an evangelist, a missionary of a puritanical
revival within the young religion of the Celtic Church, then about
200 years established. There is nothing in his known life and
teaching that Welshmen need feel uneasy about. He was great
in the highest spiritual sense, and a wise statesman in his dealings
with the secular and unbeliever. It is said he fought long for the
soul of the pagan Welsh chieftain of Dyfed, a certain Boia or
Voia, of Irish origin, who maintained the cult of the Druids.
He won the chieftain's people over to Christianity: Boia is said
to have been struck down by lightning (a frequent cause of death
to man and beast on this open north-west headland), or else
slaughtered by the Irish pirate Liski, whose name is perpetuated in
nearby Porth (Port) Liski.

St David disposed of the pagans, and destroyed the heretical
Pelagian movement. He re-ordered the British Church and di-
vided Wales into dioceses. He removed the see from Caerleon to
St David's (Menevia).

He was canonised by Pope Callixtus II (1119–24):—

"Roma semel quantum dat bis Menevia tantum"

Two pilgrimages to St David's shrine henceforth were accepted
as equivalent to one to Rome.

Another Pembrokeshire-born saint was Teilo, to whom

Llandilo or Llanteilo in Carmarthenshire and Landeloy near St David's are dedicated. He was born at Eglwys Gunniau (Gumfreston) near Tenby, and studied at Whitland with St David.

These were the men who, after the withdrawal of the Romans and their influence, zealously tended the flame of Christianity in south-west Wales, assisted locally by the minor saints who dwelt at intervals in Pembrokeshire: Tyssul, Elveis, Justinian, Devanus. This was the hour of the striking Ogham stones, Christian crosses with inscribed characters, a series of straight lines, apparently based on the Roman alphabet, usually on the edges of wood and stone. Some dozen Ogham stones exist in Pembrokeshire today, of which most also have Latin inscriptions distinct from or duplicating the wording of the Ogham characters.

Chapter II

THE LAND

The northern half of Pembrokeshire was a wall of cliff and hill against which the ice-sheet of the last glaciation, cróssing the Irish Sea, butted and ground, blocking the north flowing rivers of the county so that lakes were formed (Lakes Teify, Nevern and Manorowen). The water rose until it flowed southwards over the watershed into the western Cleddau. When the ice retreated the northern rivers resumed their old courses, and the bare rocks of the north coast stood up, ice-scarred, much as they are today. The land of Pembrokeshire was already formed; this mountainous northern half contained rock of the Primary, pre-Cambrian, Cambrian and Ordovician or Silurian series: muddy shales with here and there igneous rocks; but the level southern plain, as the geological maps show, is almost simplified into alternate deposits of old red sandstone and carboniferous limestone, both highly fertile—although older and younger rocks protrude.

The Prescelly Mountains dominate the whole county; from their brown-green slopes run the clear streams which fall into the drowned Cleddau valley, the upper reaches of Milford Haven. Before they have ceased to leap and babble over their narrow rocky beds, before they can be dignified into rivers proper, the salt tide engulfs them at high water. These mountains are gentle, as smooth and green as the South Downs, hardly averaging a thousand feet high, and the highest, Prescelly Top (Foel-cwm-cerwyn), is exactly one-third of a mile above sea-level, 1,760 feet. From here on a clear day the hills of Wicklow in Eire, Bardsey Island, the Rivals and Snowdon in North Wales, and Devon with Lundy Island, are seen with a turn of the head.

The geological map shows the east-west trend of the youngest rock of all, the anthracite coal measure which occupies the syncline right across the county from Saundersfoot Bay to St Bride's Bay. It was of old worked by means of level or slope

13

cuttings through which was removed the anthracite near the surface. In George Owen's time this "smokeless cole" was mined by pickaxe and candlelight, the miners working twelve hours a day, less one hour at noon to eat bread and beer. These surface veins or "slatches" were soon worked out. Deep-mining was carried out in the nineteenth century, even under the sea at both extremities of the vein; but of late years and since the coal industry has been nationalised, the last Pembrokeshire mines have been declared unprofitable and are closed, and now lie waterlogged and derelict.

The best soil, richest agriculturally, overlies the red sandstone and carboniferous limestone of the south, and this southern part also has the mildest and driest climate not only of the county but of all western Wales. The Castlemartin headlands and the low island of Skokholm have only 35 inches of rain annually, which is close to the figure for the Isles of Scilly, south Cornwall and Jersey. But the rainfall rises sharply eastwards and inland, over 40 inches at Tenby and Haverfordwest, and over 60 inches on the Prescelly Mountains. The average number of days on which rain falls in an average parish in Pembrokeshire is just over 200 out of the year's 365.

Temperature is equable, never very hot in summer, nor cold in winter. Frost on the coast is comparatively rare. In the phenological report for 1934, published in the *Quarterly Journal of the Royal Meteorological Society*, is a map showing the average floral isophenes (lines of equal flowering dates for twelve selected plants) for thirty-five years from 1891 to 1925, of the British Isles: these lines indicate that spring flowers bloom earlier in south Pembrokeshire than anywhere else on the mainland of England and Wales.

At the same time, although winter is mild and spring early, summer is never as warm as in the same latitude inland. Atlantic water surrounds Pembrokeshire as a thermal jacket; the average July temperature is only 16° F above that of January, and the extreme range between winter and summer only 44° F.

The spring is dry and sunny as a rule, often causing anxiety to the early potato growers who look for heavy late April showers to swell and bulk their crop planted early in March. The late autumn, October to December, are the wettest, and January and February the coldest, months.

Wind is mostly enemy and sometimes friend to the people of Pembrokeshire. Great gales blow at intervals between the first of October and the end of March. The most violent on record, exceeding that of a West Indies typhoon, occurred on the night of November 29th, 1954. The anemometer at Brawdy Naval Air Station, near St David's, registered its limit that night—130 m.p.h.; while that at St Ann's Head reached above 110 m.p.h. Ships were wrecked, and houses and barns unroofed, and every tree-lined road completely blocked by wind-felled trees. I well remember that hurricane, when the great fortress-like walls of Orielton trembled, and trees crashed like ninepins all through the night. Yet by report this was a local typhoon, not experienced elsewhere to the same extent in Wales. Gales of between 60 and 80 m.p.h. are more normal in Pembrokeshire.

Depressions approaching from the Atlantic are heralded by south-east winds which in a few hours bring heavy rain. This is blown away quickly by a veering wind which may pass through south to end in a stiff north-west gale, presently dying to a brief calm. Then the wind backs quietly to south-east again for the next blow. The prevailing winds lie between south-east and north-west. Anticyclones bring winds from the north and east, often from north-east; these winds are cold in winter and warm in summer.

Trees on the open coast are non-existent or stunted and bent almost double by incessant wind. This open country, dressed by the salt of the sea-wind, is better for corn and arable crops than the more sheltered inland and valley fields: to that extent wind is an ally of the farmer, but little else is it of use to man except perhaps to the tourist who likes to feel the salt on his cheek and to admire the appearance of the Severn Sea in a gale.

Wind in the winter can blast the luxuriant lattermath grass of cliffside fields, where sheep and beef cattle thrive in summer in a temperate air almost free of the annoyance of cattle flies, warble flies and other winged insect pests which frequent more sheltered inland fields. Some of the finest beasts to reach Haver-fordwest cattle market have come straight from Skomer and Ramsey Islands, where they have fattened on rough grazing and heather with no artificial feeding.

The island grazing was important as far back as Norman times, when the "agistment" of the islands had its value in the Minis-terial Accounts. And it is clear that even before the advent of the Normans, the Pembrokeshire mainland was largely pastoral, for the Celtic people were semi-nomadic graziers, under the tribal system peculiar to Wales. The cattle were the chief source of wealth of the groups of families which occupied the Pembroke-shire settlements (gwelys) under the headman (uchelwyr). Some-times a powerful nobleman or uchelwyr was the son of, or became, a petty prince, perhaps by marriage to the daughter of a neighbouring chieftain, more often by right of might in tribal raids (Giraldus Cambrensis wrote that a Welshman loves his brother best when he is dead). The land was for the common use of the community, but land tenure and certain rights were later handed down by inheritance as the country became more populated. Prince Hywel Dda (Howell the Good, died 950 A.D.) codified a system of tenure which included the law of gavel-kind by which land was passed from the father to each of his sons equally. This resulted in the division of fields and plowlands into narrowing strips, each held by a related but separate house-hold. The system, which is still in force in certain parts of western Europe, including Brittany, meant wastage of ground in excessive verges, of effort in travelling between the widely dispersed inherited plots, and of energy in boundary disputes. Hywel Dda lists as domesticated animals the horse, oxen, pig, sheep, goat, goose, chicken and bee. Wild animals include the wolf and the beaver. Wheat, barley and oats were cut with the scythe.

In spite of Viking raids and the internecine warfare of the Welsh princes, the settlement of Pembrokeshire was proceeding steadily with the growth of the population of christianised Welsh. The presence of the itinerant bards in the gwelys, we are told, indicated the progress of Welsh culture. Then came the Normans with their manorial system of land management. Those of the

16

The Green Bridge of Wales—a limestone arch on the south coast

Welsh who did not flee to the harsh uncoveted hillsides became tenants of their native soil only at the will of the Norman lord, instead of holding it by arrangement with their tribal head-man, the uchelwyr, who was a receiver of rents or dues on behalf of the community rather than for his personal benefit (and he had a responsibility in return to see that the harvest was fairly shared out among his people).

In north Pembrokeshire—Newport and St David's—the Welsh system of land tenure was less modified than in the south, where the Norman conquerors, coveting the richer level plain, extirpated, enslaved or drove forth the Welsh farmers. Gerald of Manorbier gives us a glimpse of the way of the Welshman's life in Norman times in his *Description of Wales*, published in 1194. The Welsh, he reports, were a pastoral people, with no liking for agriculture. They ate more flesh than corn. They were frugal yet hospitable. They wore rough clothes, yet beggars were unknown. Their homes were humble. They sat on rushes or hay, and slept upon beds of the same, covered with coarse-woven cloth. Three people shared one wooden platter in which *cawl* or broth was poured, made of sweet herbs and chopped meat. Every day a flat bread loaf was baked, the ancestor of the present *bara plank*, or girdle bread of Welsh farms. There was no cloth upon the table.

The land was ploughed with two or four oxen, or two oxen and two horses, the ploughman leading the team by walking backwards before the yoke. The Welshman was not particular, Gerald declared, about cheating his neighbour or brother, and would remove or transfer land-marks to his own advantage— with much ensuing litigation.

He would not marry a woman until he was sure she was capable of becoming "the joyful mother of children", a custom observed well into the present century in some of the more remote farms in the county. "The young farmer or farm hand may have access to his sweetheart of a Saturday or Sunday night, the parents of the young woman retiring to bed and leaving the warm kitchen with its perpetual culm fire, and the stairs clear for the courtship of an approved suitor, who may stay until it is close upon milking time

A pilgrimage to St David's—from a misericord in the cathedral

next morning. The week-end is chosen for the good reason that on Saturday the young man has had his weekly shave and, like the young woman, will be wearing his best clothes and be free from farm duties. The young man, having been accepted by both parents and daughter, realises that he must marry the girl if she becomes pregnant; and he does so joyfully in expectation of setting up home with the mother of the unborn children upon whom he will depend for cheap labour on his farm when his need is greatest. As they grow strong enough his children will work, often without wages, to build up the farm. Their reward comes later, when they wish to marry: they will each be given money or goods." (I quote from the 1957 edition of this book.)

The Norman lord, with his fortified manor, fish pond, columbarium (from which hundreds of pigeons were loosed to feed at will on tenants' crops), and harsh obligations and absolute rule imposed on his tenants, prevailed for three long centuries in south Pembrokeshire, and made a permanent mark on the land husbandry. Illustrating this there is extant a highly interesting "Extent of the Lands and Rents of the Lord Bishop" of St David's, said to have been compiled in 1326. The square measure of land was in "bovate" (seven acres) and "carucate" (eighty acres) and "knight's fee" (about one square mile). The chief crops were, as in Gerald's time, wheat, barley and oats, with some peas, beans and buckwheat (imported from the Holy Land), grown on twice-ploughed land.

The houses were of wood or of stone, with thatched roofs. The tenants performed numerous unpaid services and paid taxes to the bishop, who held lands and residences (minor palaces used by the bishop also as hunting lodge and law courts) at Lawhaden and Lamphey as well as St David's. They must repair the bishops' mills, carry new grindstones there, spend days grinding his corn and carrying the flour to the bishop's other baking ovens, also wine to Tenby and Carew; and there is mention of the compulsory transport of coal (anthracite) for burning limestones to make lime for the land. Weirs for the salmon fishery must be kept in good repair. Movement of heavy building material requiring the use of more than one horse was the duty of Lamphey tenants. The bishop was mighty in material, as well as spiritual, strength over his diocese. His poorer subjects carried a heavy burden of duty towards him.

For another two hundred years to the day of George Owen the agriculture was little altered: Norman feudalism in the rich south, mixed with Welsh gavelkind custom in the poor hills and bogs of the north. George Owen was perhaps unduly full of praise of the quality of Pembrokeshire's soil for agriculture. The winter wheat of the south of the county was good and plentiful enough to be exported to France, Spain and Ireland. In the north oats were grown without change year after year until the land was exhausted.

George Owen's account "of the maner of husbandrie & tillage of the lande, & of the naturall helpe & amendements the soile it selfe yealdeth, for betteringe and Mendinge the lande as lyme, two kinds of Marlesand woase [ooze] or oade [weed] of the sea" is of deep interest to the student of the history of agricultural land management. Some of the usages he describes are still practised in Pembrokeshire, though with modern mechanical aids, as that of liming. In Owen's day limestone was burned between layers of anthracite in small kilns, of which a great number exist, disused, in the county today in most inland villages, and along the coast in each bay which at high tide could take a small ship loaded with broken limestones and anthracite; also on the islands of Caldey, Skokholm, Skomer and Ramsey. This stone was hewn from the limestone outcrops in the south of the county.

There were no other "artificial" fertilisers then. The burned lime was carted to the fields from the kiln; when the heaps were slaked by rain and dew to a powdery consistency they were ready for spreading with a shovel. Lime was most needed on the non-limestone land of the centre and north of the county. The raw lime, deposited in heaps in the fields, was popular in north Pembrokeshire, but nowadays spreading is done mechanically direct from the lorry loaded at the quarry.

Marling or claying of light land, and sanding of heavy land, was practised, the sand coming from the shore and being good for manuring barley. Seaweed was gathered and laid in heaps to rot before being spread on the land, as it is in the Channel Islands and the Isles of Scilly today. Some poor land, with heath and rough turf, had its humus carpet pared and burnt ("bettinge and burninge") and the ashes strewn over the bare subsoil—"ill husbandrie, wherein they were much to be blamed in doinge themselves, the lande and the Countrie, harme", comments Owen, and rightly.

Cattle, horses and sheep were often folded on grass at night in the summer, behind hurdles, to make them dung land selected for ploughing. On this manured plot in the next year oats were grown and for as many years after until the land became barren —a bad practice George Owen declared, for even "one cropp of oates pulled down the pride of good grounde verye low".

Normally sheep were allowed to roam over the whole parish in winter, without shepherding, each sheep being marked, but large flock owners were apt to use a dozen marks and were not above altering marks on other sheep to their personal advantage. There was a great lack of enclosures in Owen's day, and he complains that more than three thousand young people were employed in Pembrokeshire herding cattle and horses, which he regarded as bad for their minds and bodies, as encouraging idleness.

Local markets for the disposal of cattle on the hoof were confined to the annual local fairs, and this was a great drawback to the poorer farmers who could not sell cattle for cash locally more than once a year and had to have credit from moneylenders. Cattle—chiefly Welsh blacks—were driven out of Pembrokeshire by road to the English markets, to be fattened by English farmers.

Haverfordwest on Saturday was the chief market of the county, and disposed of plenty of first-class beef, mutton, pork, bacon, veal, goose, capon, kid, lamb, rabbit, turkey and all kinds of poultry, and wild fowl and fish in season. Pembroke market was also on Saturday. Tenby had a daily market for fish.

In 1794 Charles Hassall compiled "A General View of the Agriculture of Pembroke" for the Board of Agriculture. He found the farmers backward compared to those in England, decided that Pembrokeshire was not well suited to the growing of corn, and advocated a reduction of tillage in favour of grass. In two hundred years much of the land had been enclosed and improved. One hundred years later, in the 1890s, there was a deep agricultural depression, and the area of cultivated land had fallen by a third. Many labourers and farmers emigrated to the New World, and landlords began to sell their large farming estates. Prosperity did not return to Pembrokeshire until the First World War broke out. For a while, then, farmers made money, but by 1930 another depression had set in, and farm prices were disastrously low. It took a Second World War to put the farmers back on their feet, by which time marketing schemes and boards were helping to regulate and market agricultural production as we know it today.

In Pembrokeshire at the moment most coastwise farms are laid down to fifty per cent arable and forty per cent short ley, with perhaps ten per cent permanent pasture—this last is generally the home meadow close to the house and buildings. The arable rotation is often early potatoes the first and perhaps second years, sometimes with sugar beet or broccoli in the same year when the potatoes are out in June, then three corn crops, the last undersown with a three-years' lay. This sequence may be varied, and usually is, depending upon the price of early potatoes, broccoli and sugar-beet. But horn and corn remain as the basis of the coastwise farming economy. Hereford cattle or a white-face cross are reared on nurse-cows in the fields and brought in to fatten in winter yards in their third year (unless sold earlier as store cattle on the poorer farms). The muck made in these yards is carried to the stubbles of the third corn crop as a rule.

Oats twice, followed by barley with ley seeds, used to be the corn rotation, but again this is varied today, and the grass and clover may be laid down in spring on its own to ensure a full cover.

During the years of depression following the First World War when corn prices reached rock bottom many farms turned to milk production because of the guaranteed prices offered by the Milk Marketing Board. The majority of small farms inland and many on the coast now produce milk, and have reduced their arable acreage to a minimum. Kale and some silage is grown on these holdings, where grass is the main crop. The sheltered inland valley farms, with a high rainfall, are well suited to grass production. Milk farmers have prospered during the last twenty years, as can be seen by the improving condition of their homes and farms. The work, however, is unremitting, seven days a week, and any prosperity is well deserved. Milk production is no fool's sinecure—skill and hard work are required to maintain production at a profitable level, and safeguard the health of the herd. Fortunately Pembrokeshire cattle have always been healthy: the whole of west Wales is now declared free of bovine tuberculosis. Milk herds continue to increase: in the year ending September 30th, 1955, milk sales reached a record peak of nearly 26 million gallons.

Sheep are kept on most farms: on the larger farms of the south the favourite breeds are black faced—Clun Forest and Suffolk types predominate; lately Cheviot and Down Sheep have been used, and the Dorset Horn ram is popular for crossing. In the north Welsh sheep are kept on the Prescelly mountains, a subsidy on the use of pure-bred Welsh rams being paid by the Ministry of Agriculture. These restless Welsh sheep are hard to contain when brought into lowland fields. Farmers on the intermediate foothill land in the north like to keep a less agile breed for this reason; and for the production of larger carcases a Welsh cross is common. Many Welsh mountain ewes are drafted for sale to lowland and English border counties after they have had their third lamb, and they are then turned to a heavy breed ram, and sold fat in the autumn with their half-breed lambs. On the whole the Pembrokeshire Welsh Mountain ewe is rather heavier and in better condition than her counterpart in the mountainous interior of Cardiganshire and Carmarthenshire where the rainfall is high and the temperature lower: these lean inland sheep improve visibly on coming to the coastal hills.

Sheep have steadily declined in numbers within the last fifty years in Pembrokeshire; they have been under the 100-thousand mark for the last ten years. Farm horses are rapidly disappearing, and are now fewer than one per thousand acres of farmland. There is a limited demand for riding and hunting horses, which are bred by the service of a travelling thoroughbred stallion.

On the Prescelly Mountains a strong rather heavier type of the red-brown Welsh mountain pony is present in a herd of brood mares and two or three stallions running free. The foals are rounded up and ear-marked each autumn, and surplus two-, three- and four-year-old animals are sold, some after being broken and trained for riding—they are ideal for children. Some hill farmers still use them to ride when shepherding.

Pigs and poultry fluctuate in numbers as elsewhere, something like 15 thousand pigs and half a million of all poultry being an average figure over the last twenty years. As to breeds, the Large White pig as a favourite is suffering from competition with the Welsh. There are other breeds but in small supply. The present tendency is for the Welsh, improved by the use of Landrace boars, to supplant the Large White. The Welsh-Landrace first-cross produces an early maturing bacon pig with fine joints and lean flesh, inheriting its bacon qualities from the Landrace, and health and hardihood from the Welsh.

There is an increasing and successful development of poultry as an important side-line to farming, especially on the medium- and smaller-sized farms. Old buildings are being adapted and new ones erected to house "deep-litter" hen flocks which are fed intensively on proprietary foods, supplemented with home-grown cereals where available. The eggs are sold locally or collected by the main dairies maintaining egg-packing stations, and many eggs go to supply hatcheries in the season.

Turkeys have become a profitable line on a few farms. Intensive methods here again have given good returns, the poults being reared indoors. Nor is it entirely a Christmas market that is catered for. A few farmers rear and despatch to market young turkeys in prime table condition over nine months of the year. The production of table chickens, from petits poussins to large capons, is also undertaken; but that of geese and ducks for the table is on a declining scale, although formerly Pembrokeshire was noted for the number of "green" or Michaelmas geese on the farms and commons.

Packs of foxhounds have existed for some hundreds of years in the county. At present the Pembrokeshire Foxhounds operate from kennels near Haverfordwest, covering the centre and north of the county. The South Pembrokeshire Foxhounds hunt the southern half, from kennels at Cresselly. A pack of otter-hounds is kept at St Clears, just over the boundary in Carmarthenshire, and visits Pembrokeshire rivers—the Nevern, Gwaun, Taf, Cleddau and Ritec (Tenby Marsh).

CHAPTER III

THE PEOPLE

THE history of the "natives" of Pembrokeshire is bound up in the story of the many invaders who arrived by sea. The Megalithic dolmen-builders from the Mediterranean who about 2000 B.C. left their monuments along the east and west shores of the Irish Sea were the forerunners if not the forefathers of both the coastal Welsh and of the Irishmen who brought Christianity by sea from southern Ireland to the headlands of Pembrokeshire in the last years of the Roman occupation of Britain. St David's, the nearest southern headland to Ireland, was a chief point of departure and arrival, and it is significant that its "Vallis Rosina" became the site of one of the first monastic settlements in Wales.

Probably the Irish Deisi tribes which appear to have colonised Pembrokeshire some two hundred years before the birth of St David have had some influence on the related language of the native Welsh. Traffic was frequent across St George's Channel during the lifetime of St David and during the ensuing two or three centuries: not only were priests moving about, but trade was brisk. There was gold in south-eastern Ireland at that time.

The Viking rovers now began to raid Ireland, and to form settlements. From these bases in the ninth century they extended operations to Wales, and for another hundred years they plundered Pembrokeshire at intervals. What had now become the shrine of St David in Vallis Rosina was sacked and burned, more than once. One often-quoted visit of the Scandinavian pirates was that of Hubba, who is said to have brought twenty-three ships of war to winter in the safety of Milford Haven in A.D. 877–878. From him the village of Hubberston evidently acquired its name: it may have been an important first permanent settlement of the Scandinavians, whose influence is obvious in many present-day place-names along the coast. Ramsey, Grassholm, Skokholm, Skomer and Caldey Islands are all names of Scandinavian origin: as also Haverfordwest, Milford, Herbrandston, Harold-ston, Hasguard, Hundleton, Stack Rocks, Studdock, Fishguard, Tenby (Dane-by) and others which lie especially along the shore and inland on the north side of Milford Haven.

These settlements could only have been achieved by conquering or driving out the Irish-Welsh natives. The Norse language was incomprehensible to the Welsh, who remained unabsorbed in the wild northern half of the county, an inland people with little or no knowledge of the sea. They had boats, it is true, in the form of coracles—saucer-like waterproofed lath-and-hide canoes—but fit only for the inshore fishing and for rowing upon rivers where salmon run.

An uneasy peace descended upon Pembrokeshire round about the year 1000 A.D. with the Scandinavians occupying the sea-way of Milford Haven and the peninsular lands of both shores thereof. The Welsh seem to have stood their ground in most of the north of the county as well as in that part of the south-west known later as the hundred of Castlemartin.

This truce was broken by the arrival of descendants of the Norsemen, the Normans, who came both by sea and by land: they had already won from the Welsh much of southern Glamor-ganshire, whose Gower coast throws a long arm in sight of the Tenby shore. One Arnulph de Montgomery and his men sailed up the Haven and, avoiding the northern shore already occupied by their Norse kinsmen, seized upon the almost enisled rock at Pembroke, on which they built a palisade camp of stake and earth.

This first simple fort was later altered to make the beginnings of the present fine castle of Pembroke. From Pembroke the Normans overran all south Pembrokeshire to beyond the present Carmarthenshire boundary, to Laugharne and Llanstephan, and in the succeeding two centuries they erected the chain of castles marking the Landsker, the boundary of hill and bog behind which the native Welsh held their own in the poorest region agricultur-ally. These castles are from east to west: Roch, Haverfordwest, Picton, Wiston, Lawhaden, Narberth, Carew, Amroth, Laugharne and Llanstephan. Only Picton and Amroth are used as residences today. Pembroke castle remained the centre bastion of the Norman settlement.

The Welsh disappeared from within this southern ring of fortifications. The Welsh tongue was no longer spoken, and only Norman or Anglo-Saxon English was heard from Haverfordwest to the Bristol Channel. The Norsemen speaking a dialectic Norse no doubt could understand fairly well the Latinised-Anglicised version of Norse brought by the Normans.

It is interesting to note that even today much of the Landsker is waste land and spread over a chain of large parishes, indicating that for centuries it was agriculturally sterile because it was a disputed frontier and a battle-ground.

These races of Celtic and Norse-Norman peoples were the foundation of the present distinct races of Pembrokeshire people. Like oil and water they did not mix successfully, and they have retained their different properties and characters down the centuries. The north Pembrokeshire Welsh homes were and are still humble dwellings and small farms with rough pastures: and the south Pembrokeshire English homes were stone-built manors, many of them today metamorphosed into substantial farmhouses with stock-yards standing foursquare like miniature fortresses.

The Celts of the north worshipped in little steepleless churches carrying a single bell in an open arch above the roof. The southern English erected substantial churches with very tall square battlemented towers which often carried a number of bells and which served as military look-outs against the marauding Welsh. A map of churches in Pembrokeshire clearly shows the ethnic division.

The Norman overlords employed a retinue of Saxon-English labour and armed men recruited from long-conquered lands in England. Early during the twelfth century these were reinforced by the importation of Flemings who had been rendered homeless by the inundations of the low-lying Flanders coast. King Henry I, hearing of these refugees from his European lands, sent a large number to Pembrokeshire. Subsequently further batches of Flemings were sent to the county during the reign of Henry II. In fact these colonists, hard-working and apt in many trades, including that of seamen, established a thriving sea-traffic between south Wales and their homeland in the Low Country and brought with them many commodities, including wine. The manufacture of cloth from the wool of their pastoral flocks led to an export trade: the relics of this once booming profession may be seen in the few wool mills which survive in Pembrokeshire.

The language of these labouring class Flemings did not differ greatly from and was soon absorbed in that of the Norman English: but some rural Frisian and German words survive in the south Pembrokeshire dialect to this day. In his comprehensive book Laws gives a full list of the unusual words or idioms in the current dialect which may be heard in the country, village and small towns of Little England beyond Wales.

The Flemings were successful colonists, amassed wealth, and rose to responsible positions in local government. They took over some of the manors and great farms, even castles (Roch and Wiston), and gave money to support the church and its establishments (Monkton Priory, St David's Hospital, the Knights of St John at Slebech). They formed a strong home guard army in south Pembrokeshire and loyally answered the not infrequent summons to aid the King against the Welsh princes who frequently descended upon Pembrokeshire, raiding, looting and burning. They learned to fear and so to hate the Welsh. To this day the south Pembrokeshire man has no great liking for his northern neighbour, and is apt to speak contemptuously of the people living "up in the Welsh", and to accompany the phrase with a flick of the thumb over the shoulder and a wry grimace.

Two world wars and the permanent settlement in both north and south Pembrokeshire of War Department establishments, with their disruptive influence on local communications and customs, have tended to break the ethnic barrier. Marriages between Welsh and English are less infrequent. While few south Pembrokeshire farming men can be induced to take over north Pembrokeshire land, Welshmen from the north are more ready, when opportunity allows, to "come south" and farm a richer soil in a milder climate. A study of the registers of electors in southern parishes over the last fifty years has shown that more and more of the Jones, Williams, Davies, Evans and Thomas tribes are filling the lists, and fewer of the picturesque variety of English country names, such as Allen, Skyrme, Greenslade, Hathaway, Mirehouse, Warlow, Belton, Beynon, White, etc., appear.

Welsh is still the language spoken by the old and by the young in the homes of the north, especially away from the coast where the influence of English, the language of trade and tourism, is so powerful. The north Pembrokeshire hill farming family speaks Welsh exclusively at home, and yet even here, there is a tendency of the adolescents, who go forth to work at trades (at sea, or in garages, shops, hotels and W.D. establishments), to consider their native language as old-fashioned, out-of-date, and of no advantage to their careers. Between the ages of fifteen and forty, perhaps, the Welsh-born Pembrokeshire male and female are inclined to despise their own language. With ripeness comes wisdom, and older people, remembering the language of infancy, often return to their Welsh ways wholeheartedly—occasionally, as if to make up for the neglect, to extreme Nationalism.

In the south the average man and woman is proud of being English, or at least anxious to be considered so. Judged by the standard of cultured London or commercial English, their English has a pronounced soft lilting accent, very pleasing to some ears, but often dubbed to their disadvantage as "Welshy" by those who interview them for employment in England.

Nothing much more need be said of the outward distinguishing characteristics of the two races inhabiting Pembrokeshire. But as to character the Welsh are more cautious, introspective (not to say inhibited), dour and reserved, as befits a race inhabiting the poorest land in the county, where conditions of soil and climate are more rigorous. They have outwardly a stricter religious code, attend principally chapels, and do no work on Sundays. They drink less intoxicating liquor. They are better singers. They live simply and efficiently on land where an Englishman might starve. They are suspicious of trading with an Englishman, from a long history of exploitation of Welsh resources and markets by English capital. They are often contemptuous of English buyers who will not haggle over a sale. They love to believe that they have got the best of the bargaining, which on their part they are prepared to carry on all day—for they are tenacious and will get the last penny if they can. Time never seems important to them, yet they are early risers, and hard workers on their own, and quick and efficient as employees.

The south Pembrokeshire English are undoubtedly more open-hearted, smiling, easy-going, even indolent. They like music but sing badly. They talk excessively, and go less to church and chapel. They drink much, are amiable when drunk. They are fond of children and animals. Illegitimate children, once numerous, were not regarded with disfavour. All of which has been put down by some observers to existence on a richer, more amenable soil in a happier enervating climate.

Both races of countrymen have (to me as a mixture of both) certain traits in common: willingness to help without expectation of reward; inability to say no even when asked to do something they have no intention of doing; and lack of time sense which results either in failure to keep appointments, or late arrival at place of same. These characteristics have been noted in the people of southern Ireland, from whence, as we have seen, the Deisi tribes settled in Pembrokeshire. The two peoples still have many traits in common. Ever since the arrival of the Deisi, in fact, the Irish have come east to Pembrokeshire—although there has been little movement in the opposite direction since Ireland was conquered by Strongbow and Fitz Stephen in the twelfth century.

About the years 1523-4 some 20 thousand Irishmen, descendants of the followers of the Norman conquerors, flooded Pembrokeshire to such an extent that complaints were laid before the King (who was also Earl of Pembroke) of the way these immigrants disturbed the peace, and by their very numbers assumed control of the local councils, and acted riotously, as "Raskells", claiming kindred with Pembrokeshire families.

Irish labourers, attracted by higher rates of pay, are still coming here, and marrying Pembrokeshire women, or bringing over Irish wives, to settle down in the county, convenient for a return visit to "the old people" across the water.

The late Rev. Baring-Gould, who lived at Haverfordwest,

collected a great deal of the folk-lore of Pembrokeshire people. Quaint customs are remembered today, but their practice is dying out. "Mari Llwyd" (also practised elsewhere in Wales) required a horse's skull, bedecked with ribbons, which was worn by a man who, accompanied by other singers, serenaded from house to house just before Christmas. The Guisers, with their dramatics, were evidently a survival of the Middle Age Mystery Plays. In Tenby these took the form, among the fishermen, of dressing one man up as "The Lord Mayor of Penniless Cove". He wore a mask and flowers or ribbons, and was carried in a chair by attendants with flags and violins. He blessed each house that yielded the party something for Christmas.

The New Year would be seen in by parades of singers in the streets, followed by a torchlight procession to church for the first service of the year—the procession would start from the Rector's house, and return to it afterwards.

Miss M. Wight has kindly given me permission to quote from her book on Pembrokeshire in which she describes how children went

"round from house to house, and stop all whom they meet in the streets offering to sprinkle them—for pennies of course— with the water that they are carrying in cups. Sprigs of some evergreen, box, rosemary or sea spurge may be used as sprink- lers. Today this is done 'for luck', but it must be a survival of some definite ceremony. Probably it harks back to the Asperges, or Holy Water, of the Catholic Church, but that again can be traced back to some far earlier pagan ritual, probably a charm to produce rain and so fertility. There is a traditional song to accompany the sprinkling, which begins:

'Here we bring new water from the well so clear;
For to worship God with, this happy New Year;
Sing levy dew, sing levy dew, the water and the wine,
With seven bright gold wires and bugles that do whine;
Sing reign of fair maid with gold upon her toe,
Open you the west door and turn the old year go;
Sing reign of fair maid with gold upon her chin,
Open you the east door and let the New Year in.'

"Here is surely food for the folk-lorist's speculations. There seems to be a general belief in Wales and the west of England that water drawn from any well in the first dawn of a New Year has very special virtues, while the holy wells were especially full of power at that time. Even to rise early on New Year's day was in Pembrokeshire considered luck-bringing. Another south Pembrokeshire song for this day runs thus:

'Get up on New Year's morning,
The cocks are all a-crowing;
And if you think you're awake too soon,
Why, get up and look at the stars and moon.
The roads are very dirty
My shoes are very thin;
I wish you a happy New Year,
And please to let me in.'

"Good Friday also had its ancient customs. It is said that in the Englishery reeds were gathered and woven into the form of a man, fixed upon a wooden cross and laid in a field; this was called 'Making Christ's Bed'. Until the end of the eighteenth century, people in Tenby walked barefoot to church on Good Friday, 'so as not to disturb the earth'; this is said to have been a pre-Reformation custom. Hot cross buns were eaten, and some of them hung up in the kitchen till the following year; these were thought to have healing virtues and to frighten away evil spirits.

"St Stephen's Day had its proper customs: boys chased girls with boughs of holly, whipping them savagely on their bare arms, presumably in memory of the first martyr! On the same day, or at any time between Christmas and Twelfth Night might have been met the procession of the Cutty Wren. An unfortunate wren was caught and imprisoned in a small glass box, decorated with ribbons and carried round the town on sticks like a miniature sedan chair, of course to beg for largesse, while a long ballad was sung; a cruel custom which it is hoped is now extinct." It is.

"In Vallis Rosina"—St David's Cathedral from the east. On the left the ruins of the bishop's palace. On the right, those of St Mary's College

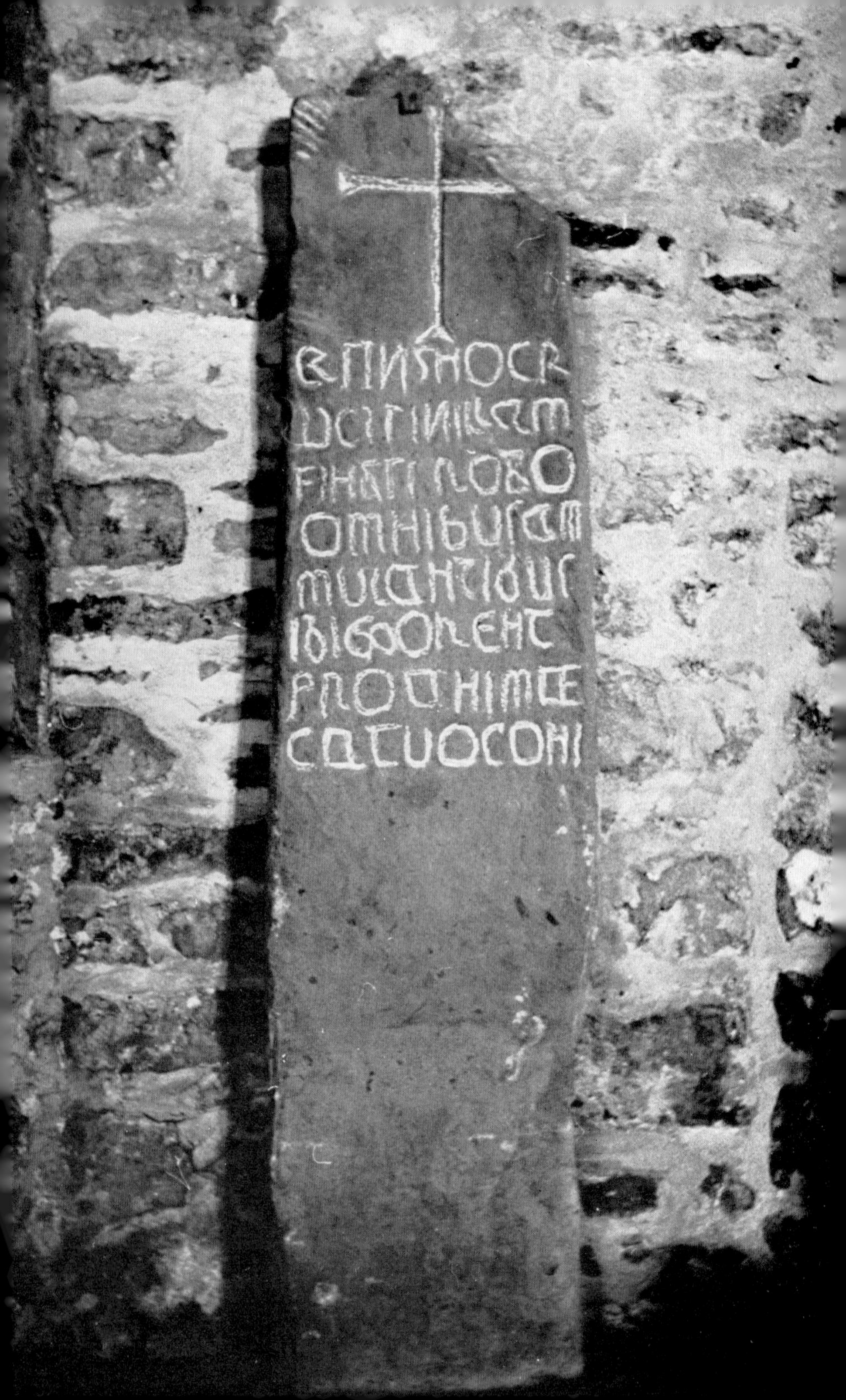

CHAPTER IV

THE SOUTHERN SHORE

ONE morning early in April I set out to map the coast path of Pembrokeshire for the National Parks Commission. It was showery, with a cool north wind blowing from the land, but when the sun gleamed on wet sand and cliff and grass the southern slope was warm and full of the promise of spring. My survey began on the south-east coast, where the over-large county of Carmarthenshire has, according to the oft-quoted chronicler George Owen of Henllys, filched the fair lands formerly belonging to the little county of Pembrokeshire, whose natural boundary hereabouts ought (one would agree after a glance at the map) to continue to be the river Taf, as it is farther inland.

Here, upon the golden sands of Pendine, I was alone with a flock of handsome oyster-catchers, I eager to explore, they to digest their heavy meal of cockles, for which the flats are famous. Behind me was the now deserted but once famous strand of firm sand used by racing motorists and occasional 'planes, stretching away for dune-edged miles to the ancient abandoned seaport of Laugharne.

Westwards cliffs upreared above the shady shore, and in the distance lay the broad sweep of Saundersfoot Bay, with Caldey Island marking the end of the view. Landwards the steep slope was deep red with winter-washed bracken. This wild little-inhabited coast under Marros Mountain is delightful to the eye of the naturalist and the geologist. Pushing through dense furze and over tumbled screes, I came to the lonely farm of Underhill. A kindly woman, impressed by the fact that I had come so many miles, invited me to enjoy a pot of tea and a plate of home-made bread and butter. She lingered to gossip.

Greatly refreshed I walked on by the fine dark wooded "cwm" marked on the map as Teague's Wood, with old mine-workings,

3   33

"Pray for the soul of me, Catuoconus"—an inscription in Ogham (lines on the edge of the stone) and in Latin now used by badgers, who had thrown their spoil upon that of the old levels. The coast paths were choked by giant furze and sapling trees bent by the south-west wind. Weedy cliff-fields were full of linnets. The only soul in sight was a man behind a team of horses ploughing a field yellow with buttercups.

To enter Pembrokeshire proper one must cross the infant stream by the east end of the pebble beach of Amroth. Upon this the sea, brown with sand and fretted by the late gale into a dun-coloured lacework, chattered ceaselessly.

There is an ancient inn on the boundary, known, as many old inns are, as New Inn. Here I drank thirstily with two farmers, one a small north county Welshman and the other a tall south-county or "Englishery" man. The Welshman had taken already too many glasses and this, from his natural inferiority complex in the presence of English people, made him aggressive. Seeing my great folder full of maps he hinted I might be a spy, come to check on these lonely beaches which had been used to rehearse the British landings in France in the 1939–45 war. The English-man, recognising me as "the bird-man" as he put it, surprisingly demanded an apology on my behalf. The befuddled Welshman grandiosely supplied free drinks by way of compensation, and offered me a lift in his car.

This I courteously refused. I was truly, I said, on a walking tour. But I watched his car start off with some uneasiness on its erratic course by the beach road.

Hard by, screened by the sea-bent trees and a wall, is Amroth Castle, now a guest house and farm, but formerly a house of probably Norman or earlier antiquity stood on the site. On the broad sands below gales frequently uncover the remains of the ancient forest which stretched across the Bristol Channel: you may see the great tree roots and pick up hazel nuts and deer antlers preserved by the sea and sand for hundreds of years.

The shallow sea advances each year with rough blows upon the waterfront of the village of Amroth. Cottages I can recall in-habited thirty years ago have been quite swept away: this is about the only change suffered by this unspoilt little place, whose name is said to be a corruption of Eareware.

Cliffs intervene, with a good bridle path over them, to Wiseman's Bridge, a small hamlet in a valley with the same pebble ridge and broad sands with rock pools full of shrimps and prawns, crabs and an occasional lobster. The Wiseman's Bridge Inn claims the distinction of having entertained Sir Winston Churchill who had come to see the rehearsal here in 1943 of the invasion of Normandy, when this vast beach from Pendine to Saundersfoot swarmed with soldiers, landing-craft, guns and all the paraphernalia of seaborne attack. As it happened the weather was rough for the rehearsal on Pembrokeshire's coast (as it was for the real thing in France) with the same piling up and stranding of barges and equipment.

The cliffs which once more rear up before the west-going pedestrian can be skirted by following a disused tram line which once brought anthracite from the Stepaside colliery inland to the harbour at Saundersfoot. It is worth taking the alternative cliff path which passes through the wooded grounds of Hean Castle, a modern edifice of uninspiring appearance, now the home of Lord and Lady Merthyr. This path and most of the coast path between Saundersfoot and Tenby are models of what such a path should be (thanks to the owner of the cliffs, Lord Merthyr), with neat signposts and excellent stiles.

Saundersfoot is probably the warmest village in the county, nestling as it does in this corner of Carmarthen Bay where it is shielded by the land from cold north and west winds. It was in a flourishing condition about two hundred years ago when the local anthracite veins were opened for working. Some of the shafts of these now abandoned mines run far under the sands of the shore. A harbour was built to load the anthracite for export in wooden schooners, ketches and barges, much of it going to Bristol, Ireland and France. The quay must have been ennobled then by the tall masts and topmasts of the sailing cargo-boats, which also took away the corn of which Pembrokeshire grew plenty. Most of the coal and corn at that time was carried down from mine and farm in the two-wheeled cart or "gambo", as it is called in west Wales.

The masts in Saundersfoot harbour are today puny affairs

rising from small pleasure yachts and boats. The harbour is almost silted up with mud and sand, and at low tide is unapproachable by sea. That sand however has brought prosperity in the form of tourists and visitors on summer holidays. An extensive caravan park is the means of more than doubling the winter population during the July–September holidays. Children love the sands, pools and shallow, comparatively warm sea.

Next day, after a night at the St Bride's Hotel in great comfort, I started out through Lord Merthyr's woods to Monkstone Point, with grand views from a fine easy cliff-edge path which made planning simplicity itself. From Monkstone to Tenby the way is more open, exposed to the south-west wind. The path arrives finally at a tiny open-air theatre with a pergola or temple, looking down on the remarkably beautiful harbour and water front of Tenby.

Without doubt Tenby is the most charming of all Welsh seaside towns, although with under five thousand inhabitants it scarcely merits the not altogether felicitous title of town. Its situation is romantic and superb, covering a limestone peninsula, with the island of Caldey guarding the ocean approach. The town bay faces north-east, away from prevailing winds, and is half land-locked by the jutting Castle Hill and St Catherine's Rock. Behind this the mile-long South Beach fringes the blue-green of Caldey Sound.

Formerly there was an estuary breaching this southern strand, and old paintings show that ships at high tide went far inland to Gumfreston and some say to St Florence. But since the railway crossed the valley the embankment acted as a dam, and the sand-hills increased and smothered the river Ritec, so that it now runs in an underground drain which in heavy rain cannot accommodate the swollen waters and the low land is deeply flooded. This is the Tenby Marsh, noted for its wealth of wild flowers, including a rare daffodil, acres of yellow flag, willow herb and the fascinating hanging blossoms of *noli-me-tangere* (touch-me-not).

Tenby built its prosperity upon its sea-trade—merchandise and fish. It was a fortified castle in Norman times: in *Brut y*

Tywysogion is an account of how the Welsh princes Meredudd and Rhys ap Grufudd in 1150 took the castle of "Tinbych" by surprise and slew the garrison, in revenge for the ambush which had killed their brother Cadell. They are said to have marched on Tenby from Amroth Castle across the sands, at low tide, and achieved their surprise while the sentinels were looking for an attack over the land.

From the few lines of Tenby Castle which can be traced it had a magnificent enisled position over the harbour. Now the south wall of the ancient town is the most conspicuous and imposing relic of medieval Tenby, and is kept in sound condition by its citizens.

Fish—and wool: these were the main articles of trade. The weaving industry was built up skilfully by the Flemings whom Henry I had acclimatised here from inundated Flanders after his accession in 1155. These men were a tough, tenacious breed, not to be cowed by the Welshmen or by the surrounding sea. No doubt it suited Henry's purpose to let them fight for and colonise this remote corner of Wales, where the Welsh princes were so troublesome.

These Flemings are still regarded by modern Tenby people as worthy forbears. The word Flemish is used in Tenby with pride, and sometimes misused, as when the ancient round chimneys found in the district are so designated. Round chimneys are found in Welsh Wales and many other parts of the world. Nor do Tenby people today care much about their Welsh neighbours; although often glad to accept the services of young Welsh men and women in their shops and establishments, as well as benefiting from the influx of charabancs which in summer bring loads of Welsh people from the mining valleys for a day by Tenby's fair sea and sands.

Henry IV gave Tenby a charter, so important had its trade become. In 1458 work was put in hand to strengthen the decaying walls of the town, six feet broad in every part so that the defenders could patrol them, and the moat cleansed and made thirty feet wide everywhere. "Artillerye and munyssion" were provided and for a while all was in fighting trim. But in 1588 the walls were discovered to be again in an alarming state of decay, the era of Elizabethan prosperity having evidently advanced trade and caused the citizens to neglect the fortifications.

In 1471 the Welsh-born future king, Henry Tudor, fourteen years old, escaped at Tenby for France. In this he was assisted by Thomas White, mayor and merchant, who on his return as Henry VII to power was given a lease of all the crown lands about Tenby. Tenby was ever Royalist, and consequently was besieged and suffered in the Civil Wars, when the castle and walls were finally reduced to no more than the present walls and gateways, and one or two rooms of the castle now used as a museum.

The said Thomas White lies under one of many monuments in the noble old church of St Mary in the centre of Tenby. This is interiorly one of the finest and oldest churches in Wales, with its two aisles and imposing flight of steps to the altar. It was rebuilt about 1250, probably on the site of a Celtic church; at one time Gerald the Welshman was rector. Its tall spire is a mark for ships at sea. The nave piers are curiously without capitals.

The stone-built house of a Tenby merchant of the wealthy Tudor period of about 1600 has been preserved by the National Trust. It peeps towards the harbour just below the main street, and has a so-called Flemish chimney, and a largely original Tudor interior.

On Castle Hill is Tenby Museum, housing in its two small rooms the great collection of prehistoric bones and implements taken from the limestone caves of Caldey Island and those of Hoyle's Mouth (by Tenby Marsh), and from the sunken forests exposed at low tide at Amroth, and from the sand-dunes. It is rich, too, in local shells and saltwater specimens—for at one time Philip Gosse worked here on the marine life.

Opposite Castle Hill is St Catherine's Island, a rock separated from the mainland only at high tide. It is smothered in the large yellow mesembryanthemum and other acclimatised flowering plants. A solid-looking Victorian fort has been turned into a private house, and access to the top of the island is restricted. Several plans have been made to convert St Catherine's into a show place and amusement centre, and these plans have included a bridge or an overhead wire for conveying visitors at a fee. Nothing has come of these schemes; the most appropriate one, for converting the thick-walled fort into a marine aquarium, has been delayed, but lately a small zoo has been opened there.

Many have been and will be the schemes to entice visitors and their money to Tenby. As a healthy seaside resort it seems to have attracted men from Norman times, when the Earls of Pembroke visited and stayed behind its secure walls. In the time of Fenton (1800) it began to be known as a fashionable bathing place "unrivalled by any in the principality". A certain Sir William Laxton obtained the services of the architect Cokerell to build enclosed baths:

> "for ladies and gentlemen with dressing-rooms to each; and four private cold baths for single persons. Several warm and vapour baths, with dressing-rooms tempered with warm air, and a cupping-room, are fitted with the latest improvements, and bed-rooms are provided in the bath-house for invalids. A handsome room for the bathers, their friends, and company to assemble in, is built commanding the sea and the harbour, and is provided with refreshments, so as to form a fashionable morning lounge. An excellent carriage road is formed to the bath-house, and a spacious vestible for servants to wait in, without mixing with the company."

I wonder what Fenton would think if he could see the sands in August crowded with hundreds of people bathing in the sea, and his elegant bath-houses forgotten and non-existent? Tenby is no longer exclusively fashionable with Fenton's "company of the first quality": it is the happy holiday ground of the middle-class from the Midlands and south Wales towns staying by the week, and of colliers' families and clubs arriving by coach for the day. And what a day! It is always a pleasure to see the wonder and delight in the expression on the faces of the people of the coal valleys as they walk up from the inland coach park and debouch upon the high promenade of the Norton or North Gate road, with its magnificent view of Tenby harbour and roadstead, whose curving line encloses the beautiful sandy bay lively with small boats and people. The red rocks, yellow sand, white buildings, blue sea and multicoloured sailing and motor boats delight the jaded eye, which is further refreshed by the wide view bounded by the rugged Gower coast and Caldey Island.

For these day-visitors from the smoke-grimed narrow valleys, Tenby must seem like a glimpse of heaven. I have watched with almost as much delight as theirs the wonder and content in their eyes as they basked on the sands or gossiped over tea in the cafés overlooking the sea. The more adventurous can go for a few hours to Caldey Island for a taste of salt water sprayed on their pale faces, and for a glimpse of the monastery and the monks at work on their farm—or if the weather is too bad for the crossing, there is the monastery shop in one of the side streets of Tenby, with its trinkets, scent from the island herb garden, pottery and fal-de-lals—a surprising mixture of luxuries from this substantial and down-to-earth Cistercian community. The sight of the monks on their visits to Tenby, and the presence of a monastery on the island itself are part of the charm of Tenby for many visitors and residents.

In the harbour is the lifeboat station, with occasional cruises open to the public in the fine modern motor lifeboat. The Tenby station has a long record of rescues. One I remember vividly was that of the crew of the St Govan's lightship which, in a violent midnight gale, took water and with her pumps out of action, and light extinguished, began to sink. It was a heroic achievement to bring the lifeboat alongside the waterlogged lightship in that black night gale and safely collect the entire crew; the tide races at St Govan's make the place rough on the calmest day. For this Her Majesty the Queen was to decorate the coxswain.

In the little "fishermen's" chapel close by the pier, marine men were, and are still, accustomed to attend divine service and offer thanks for "preservation from an element in whose every wave death may lie in ambush", as Fenton puts it. But there are few, a very few, real fishermen left in Tenby today. The fish, these men say, have become scarce as the result of the offshore grounds being overfished with modern gear by ocean-going trawlers; it is a more certain reward to cater for the visitors in

Manorbier Castle, birthplace of Gerald the Welshman, who described it as the fairest place in Wales
South Pembrokeshire men whose faces are said to show traces of Flemish ancestry

summer, and the boats are laid up for overhaul during the winter.

A "pool" of motor boats manages the daily ferry to and from Caldey Island, and as many as three thousand people make the voyage in a fine week. The island is closed to visitors on Sunday, when the Tenby boatmen run excursions elsewhere—to Amroth, Saundersfoot and west along the cave-worn limestone cliffs of Giltar.

There are in Tenby two cinemas, a little theatre and dance halls for evening and wet weather entertainment. If you should happen to arrive at the end of July the annual St Margaret's Fair takes place then, when for two days stalls, booths, roundabouts and "dodgems" block the South Parade under the town walls.

Tenby is in almost every aspect charming, with its wonderful views and environment, and its old-world houses and wandering narrow streets. It is to be hoped her councillors and citizens will not allow their town to be spoilt by so-called modern improvement, that her streets will remain narrow and her houses tall and white. The proposed clearing of the ugly rows of concrete-faced houses near the station would seem to provide a wonderful opportunity to build tall colour-washed blocks of flats in keeping with the older houses, and incidentally arrest the present tendency to sprawl westwards over valuable agricultural land with a rash of unimaginative and uneconomic council houses.

*   *   *   *   *

A north-westerly gale with stinging hail welcomed me as I crossed the great beach south of Tenby, and climbed the heights of Giltar Point. A farmer who took shelter in the rocks with me declared that the weather had completely changed in his lifetime of seventy years. "It's now six weeks later each year—spring, and winter—there ain't any summer to speak of, just one fox day between spring and autumn."

"It's Friday—and also the thirteenth," I reminded him. "You can't expect much on such a day."

"I'm not superstitious. All the same I likes to sow my corn and cure my bacon on a waxing moon."

41

The medieval chapel of St Govan blocks the stairway to the sea and to the holy-well used by the hermit
Low-tide by Pembroke Castle, the main fortress of the Norman conquerors of "Little England"

By the time the sleet had cleared I had gathered a lot of local folklore, told in the rich English dialect by this old man. One item concerned a "maychate" he possessed, which brought many vipers from the hill into the house. This apparently is a characteristic only of the maychate.

"What is a maychate?"

"Why, surely you know," he said full seriously. "A cat born in the month of May."

And so to Lydstep Haven, where I was again glad to shelter—this time in the modern mansion, formerly the property of a Lord St Davids and now an admirably run guest house, within a few yards of a wide pebble beach between the limestone cliffs.

Southwards is the high headland of Lydstep Point, in National Trust ownership, and beyond and beneath are the Lydstep Caverns, to be safely explored at low tide only. These and other caves along the Pembrokeshire coast are used as inaccessible roosting and nesting places by the rare chough or red-billed crow, and in some of these southern caves the grey seal cow comes ashore to bear her calf in the autumn.

The westward path skirts a military camp covering Skrinkle Farm and Old Castle Head, where the red sandstone reappears. On this headland is another and much older camp—one of many Romano-British or Iron Age settlements which occupy the peninsular points of Pembrokeshire cliffs with their double or triple raths or ramparts. The way of life of the people inhabiting these cliff castles is hinted at in the chapter on the islands.

Bypassing the complete new village and W.D. settlement at the back of Old Castle Head we come to the sandy inlet of Manorbier, with its castle majestically rising from the rock in the centre spur of the valley. Here in this Norman house was born in 1147 Gerald the Welshman, who loved Pembrokeshire so well. As a boy he built churches in these sands, prophetic of his ecclesiastical career and never-realised ambition to become a bishop. Orchards, vineyards and nut groves and fish ponds once graced the valley below the castle where now only the ruins of a mill and thickets are the home of small singing birds. There were a dovecote and a deer park. The main walls of the castle remain, and inside them is the room where it is said Gerald was born. Part of the ancient baronial suite has been converted as a habitable cottage.

Manorbier was never besieged or attacked in its long peaceful history, partly because its Norman owner, de Barri, had married a Welshwoman, grand-daughter of the powerful Prince of south Wales, Rhys ap Tewdwr, and partly because it was small, and despite Gerald's views, unimportant and out-of-the-way. The church is as old in foundation: its tower is very tall. Like many other coast-wise church towers in the county, it was used no doubt as a watch-post in times of emergency.

Gerald de Barri had everything in his favour: he was the high-born son of the daughter (sister to a bishop) of the fair Nesta, wife of Gerald de Windsor, the castellan of Pembroke; he was fair and beautiful; he possessed a remarkably assimilative brain, and as a scholar carried all before him at Gloucester Abbey and Paris University. He served at court, and held sundry livings in Oxford, Hereford and Pembrokeshire. He went to Ireland with Prince John and wrote a history of the conquest of that country. In 1188 he set out on horseback to preach the third Crusade under Archbishop Baldwin: they rode through Wales and the Welsh border. This journey, described in Latin in his *Itinerary through Wales*, with all the literary flavour he was so capable of, is most interesting reading; miracles and manifestations are numerous and an air of romance lies over the modicum of truth and propaganda. He was an ardent Catholic, and openly disapproved of the tendency for marriage among the priests of Wales; for which among other reasons he may have failed, after three visits to Rome, to secure the bishopric of St David's—too many of his would-be local supporters in the priesthood were married.

The itinerary raised some three thousand men, a goodly army in those days of small population, which were duly embarked for the Holy Land. The archbishop set off, too, but died at Acre. Gerald meanwhile joined the king's court in France.

Gerald liked to write of supernatural events. He describes the poltergeist which haunted some houses in south Pembrokeshire, including the house of Stephen Wiriet (Orielton) where a mysterious voice would upbraid those persons who were guilty of wicked and foolish acts by reciting those acts aloud before the household company.

In his fulsome praise of Manorbier he makes the naive remark that, but for the configuration of the bay, it might have been a harbour for shipping. But this south coast is very exposed to the Atlantic gales; it is subject to a twenty-five feet rise and fall of tidal water which cause violent currents under the high cliffs, especially from Stackpole Head to Linney.

Swanlake Bay, beyond Manorbier, is quiet and warm to the sun, and less visited, but Freshwater East has a wide strand sheltered from westerly gales, and is so popular with local residents that it has become rather spoiled in appearance by the erection of dozens of bungalows and summer huts and houses. But children love it, and it provides safe bathing.

The National Park coast path passes over fine unspoilt cliffs to Stackpole Quay, formerly a limestone quarry. Its mole is now used by lobster fishermen and an occasional yacht in search of temporary shelter from northerly winds.

Barafundle Bay comes next, by the path from Stackpole, a charming wild bay formerly a private bathing beach for the Cawdor family, less known than the next inlet of Broad Haven with its impressive Stack Rock—equally lovely and unspoilt. The sands of Broad Haven are accessible by car from Bosherston, by the road to Trevalen Farm.

Bosherston Lakes, formed by the blown sand damming the narrow inlet which may in prehistoric times have been a seaharbour, are famous for their summer show of water-lilies. The presence of a large ancient encampment on one spur of the limestone overlooking the water lends colour to the belief that formerly boats sailed from the Atlantic right up to the escarpment. A public path circles the southern arms of the Lakes.

Towards the northern end lay the imposing Stackpole Court, one of the homes of the Cawdor family. In the twelfth century, as Gerald relates, it was the seat of Sir Elidur de Stackpole, a Norman knight (Stackpool takes its name from the Stack Rock at the entrance to Broad Haven). There is an effigy said to be of this knight in Stackpole church, but as he wears the chain mail of a century later there is some doubt. In the Court there was a cellar with a ribbed barrel vault apparently of genuine Norman construction. Stackpole Court, recently demolished, was the scene of a bitter siege during the Civil War, but gave in to the Parliamentarians under Col. Laugharne. South Pembrokeshire has ever been of Royalist sympathies.

We now reach St Gowan's or Govan's Head with its coastguard station and magnificent carboniferous limestone cliffs. From here to Linney Head these vary between 100 and 150 feet in height and are fantastically sea-worn with caves, stacks, natural arches, blow-holes, inlets and bays. The sea-birds are numerous: razor-bills, guillemots, puffins, four breeding gulls, oyster-catchers and fulmar petrels. The raven, chough and peregrine falcon nest here, amid the more numerous jackdaws. Seals bask, cruise, dive and fish below. The turf is rich in wild flowers, including the lovely blue vernal squill, and the sea-lavender.

A whole day, or two, needs to be enjoyed in walking this stretch if you are anything of a naturalist, botanist, geologist or antiquarian. St Govan's Head is not quite accessible by car, the road from Bosherston ending at the cliff top immediately above a curious little chapel which bridges the entry to a boulder-strewn beach here.

Limestone steps (the legend goes that no one has ever accurately counted them) lead down to this tiny medieval building said to be the cell of the Arthurian knight Gawaine of the Round Table or alternatively that of St Gofen, wife of a Celtic chief. Baring-Gould may be nearer the mark in supposing him to have been the Irish Abbot of Dairinis, Gobham, contemporary with St David himself. However, as Gerald the Welshman does not refer to the chapel at all—and if it had existed he could not have failed to mention it, unless it was then a complete ruin—it was most likely built not before the thirteenth century.

In summer its situation in the little ravine is charming with its magic casement truly opening "on the foam of perilous seas in faery lands forlorn". Inside it is no more than about eighteen by twelve feet, of local stone with a slate roof well concreted down against the perilous winter gale, a bellcote, a north doorway for entrance, a south door for access to the beach, a stone altar and benches and a curious recess in the rock behind the altar. This natural water-worn recess can, by a stretch of the imagination, be viewed with the eyes of local superstition, which has it that the smoothness is due to the number of people who have entered for the purpose of framing a secret wish, which will be granted if, in the operation of turning round, you do not change your mind! But other superstitions say that the recess, which is roughly the shape of a large man, was a sanctuary for the fugitive from justice, and would close around and hide him during immediate danger.

Below the chapel is the well-preserved stone frame of the saint's well, now dry in summer possibly as the result of the undermining by the sea during recent centuries. It was notorious for its healing and wishing powers even later than Fenton's day. Crutches would be thrown aside here, and pins and pennies dropped into the water by wishful supplicants.

The westwards path skirts two great clefts; Stennis Ford and Bosherton Mere. Here is the Huntsman's Leap, by no means an impossible feat for a stout-hearted blood horse and rider, over a narrow slit in the cliff through which the sea is visible 130 feet below. Today in fact it might be leaped on foot. But the story goes that after leaping the cleft in a spirit of bravado the huntsman concerned unwisely walked back to examine the scene of his exploit, and subsequently his nerves deserted him, he never rode again, and soon died of nightmares and terror.

Caves and natural arches, with blow holes spouting foam at high tide, delight the wanderer westwards. There are at least three ancient British encampments on the peninsular headlands here, before one reaches the famous Eligug Stack Rocks.

"Eligug" is the local name for the guillemot in Pembrokeshire, obviously taken from the incessant guttural cries of these sea-birds which are massed on the top of two high limestone pillars within a stones' throw of the cliff edge near Flimston. From January to July this spectacle draws the tourist to visit, and local residents to re-visit: it is possible to drive one's car over the smooth green turf to the cliff edge and watch the massed ranks of the sea-birds without leaving one's seat. The crowns of the stacks and each broader shelf below are so thickly occupied by the guillemots that it astonishes the observer that the individual bird can recognise its own mate, egg or chick, or find room to alight. But colonial nesting birds have a wonderfully accurate sense of topographical position.

In the niches in the sheer sides of the stacks are the razorbills, which have black backs and wings in contrast with the chocolate-brown of the guillemots which are further recognisable by the more pointed bills. Still lower on the cliff the dainty little kittiwake gulls have glued their nests to mere fingerholds of rock. Above circle the herring gulls and the huge great black-backed gulls, which nest elsewhere on the cliffs but are always alert to snatch egg or chick from the smaller sea-birds.

In the last thirty years a new bird has settled on these and other Welsh cliffs; the observer at the Stack Rocks will see odd birds and pairs of the fulmar petrel sitting tamely on ledges in the cliff opposite the Stacks. In flight this petrel glides like an albatross (it is a close relative), with scarcely a flap of its pale-coloured wings. About the size and colour of a herring gull it can be recognised by this flight and by its thick short bluish bill with tubular nostrils, and dark-ringed handsome eyes. It lays only one egg and the chick remains on the ledges until September, long after the other sea-birds have departed.

Retracing our steps eastwards for a few hundred yards, it is worth while exploring minutely the peninsula of Flimston Castle, with its early British encampment with triple rampart and traces of hut-circles. The old defence works enclose the wild and beautiful Cauldron, a precipitous hole 150 feet deep connecting with the sea by arches through which sea-birds fly to their nests inside the Cauldron itself. A broad track surmounts the ancient rampart and goes down to what is sometimes called the Danish or Viking Landing, a natural rock harbour, accessible by boat in calm or offshore winds. Here, it is said, have landed in their primitive boats and currachs all the races which came by sea to colonise South Wales—the stone tomb-builders from Iberia, the Celts from mid-Europe, the first Christian saints from Ireland, the

Vikings from Scandinavia, the Normans and the Flemings; be that as it may it is more certain that, after the beginning of the long peace between Welsh and English, the little ketches and schooners of the last century docked here at high tide to collect limestones for burning, and Castlemartin corn for the coastwise trade.

Now the rough steps to the landing place no longer feel the heavy feet of labouring men and sailors laden with booty or goods. The place is sacred to the discerning visitor, the immemorial sea-birds and the seals.

From Flimston Stacks to Linney Head is one of the most deserted windswept areas in the county, uncompromising in winter, but alight with flowers and ideal for a long walk in summer. Unfortunately this whole strip of the south-west coast, from St Govan's Head to Linney, at present is often closed to the public on certain (especially week) days, when firing takes place over the area, which is a training ground for tank warfare. A little way inland the fertile limestone fields are despoiled as a result of this misuse of valuable agricultural land. The nearby farmhouses lie in ruins, shell-riddled or levelled to the ground, and ugly anti-tank bunkers have been thrown up to mar the once smiling plain. If training grounds in Wales be necessary, surely the less fertile unoccupied moors and mountains are available? It is to be hoped that pressure of the nation's food requirements will eventually lead to the restoration of the Castlemartin farms to that agricultural production which, aided by a mild dry climate and limestone soil, results in the finest corn and cattle in all Wales. Also, the white-washed farmhouses, and the hedges full of flowers, were essential ingredients in the once beautiful countryside.

As it is the visitor must be patient, turning his gaze rather upon the wonderful cliff scenery, on those days when the military gates on the Linney, Flimston and Bosherston roads are open—which they usually are on Saturdays and Sundays, and most evenings in the week.

At the extreme south-west of Pembrokeshire is the grand beach of Freshwater West, where even on fine days the thunder of

The peninsular village of Angle, in the far south-west of Pembrokeshire, consists of one long street from sea to sea

Atlantic waves is impressive, and in storm more than magnificent.
Here, if you are a strong swimmer, you may surf-ride the wild
cold waves, although a County Council notice warns you that
bathing is unsafe, due to a strong undertow present at certain
states of the tide.

Backed by wild sand-dunes, this two-mile strand was utterly
unspoilt—so far—by any development, thanks to the wise policy
of the planning department of the County Council. Against this,
but by a one vote majority, consent was recently given to the
provision of a caravan park! Certain residents make a part-time
occupation of gathering edible sea-weed, which is stored to dry
in reed-thatched huts by the shore. This is the red-brown parch-
ment-like laver-weed (*Porphyra*) which, when cooked and rolled
in oatmeal, is sold in Swansea and Cardiff as laver-bread. It is
highly nutritious and much in demand among the colliers of
south Wales, and is said to supply a deficiency in their normal
diet due to working long hours underground in the sunless coal
valleys, and to be specially good against diabetes.

And so to Angle, upon an outer isthmus of the Castlemartin
peninsula itself. The village straggles picturesquely along the
one street, east or west, with fishermen's cottages and small-
holdings. The soil and rocks are a rich red, for this is on the sandstone belt which runs right across the Haven to Dale and under
the sea to Skokholm Island. One is far from the din of main roads
and industry in the quiet haven of Angle, where the open west
beach has firm sands for children, and rock pools and islets, and the
east bay a safe harbour for small ships (being dry at low tide) and
a great expanse of flats where cockles abound. Thorne Island, a
rock offshore surmounted by a Victorian fort, is a summer guest
house accessible by small boat, and there are three inns in the
village. The main fishery is for lobsters and crabs.

This whole south peninsula of Pembrokeshire was coveted by
Norse and Norman invaders because it had "great plentie" of
corn and cattle. Here the Welsh breed of long-horned black
cattle grew so big, and deep in milk, on the rich pasture that they
were long recognised as a distinct race of the hardy Welsh mountain cattle from which they sprang. The Castlemartin Welsh

4   49

The entrance to Lawhaden Castle, the fortress residence of a Norman bishop

Blacks had their own herd book—but with the coming of the tank range and the obliteration of the farms the breed has practically disappeared. Only a remnant survives, now entered in the present Welsh Black herd book, at the Angle estate and a few other farms. Its long horns, and dual purpose nature, providing both meat and milk, have been against it in this age of specialisation, and local farmers now concentrate principally on Herefords for beef or Friesians for milk.

In the late Middle Ages down to early Victorian days this prosperous peninsula was shared between a few rich landowners, often under knights fee payable to the King. Hall in Angle was one such house; and Jestington, across the Angle flats by Rhoscrowther, another. Jestington is now Eastington Farm, but some of the walls.and one room of the late Norman structure remain.

Orielton by Pembroke was another handsome fortified house, with vast estates covering 11,000 acres; like Stackpole it has to this day in its basement and cellarage evidence of a medieval foundation. And there were many lesser houses of various vintages—some no more than glorified farmhouses—with their squires and retainers, as Bush, Corston, Lamphey and Brownslade. The tall-towered churches of the peninsula are full of interesting monuments and relics of the departed squirearchy. In few of these fine homes does the male line today go back for more than a hundred years or so, but many of the labouring people, including fishermen, claim an unbroken connection with the occupiers of the same property under the same name for many hundreds of years. Certainly some of the men and women of the roadside cottages give one the impression of being of a sturdy, broad-featured Flemish type.

CALDEY ISLAND

Much has been written already of Caldey's pre-history: of the finds, in the limestone caves, of wild animals that roamed the Bristol or Severn Channel swamps before Britain was an island; discoveries which are still being made by one or two monks living in the present Cistercian monastery, and archaeologists visiting the island.

Caldey, like St David's, is the site of an early Celtic monastery. The *Acta Sanctorum* tells of the visits of the saints there. At that time it was known (in Welsh) as Ynys Pyr or Piro, the Island of Piro, who was the first abbot of Caldey. On Piro's death by drowning in A.D. 521 Archbishop Dubricius, who happened to be in retreat on the island, appointed Samson to succeed. We know from the lives of the saints that Illtyd spent much of his time there, and St David, St Giles and St Paul de Leon were also visitors about this period.

Henry I gave the island to Robert, son of Martin de Turribus, the Norman conqueror of North Pembrokeshire, who transferred it to his mother Geva. She conveyed to the famous Benedictine monastery of St Dogmaels, near St Dogmaels. It remained a cell of that great house until the dissolution of the monasteries. It passed then to the Bradshawe family who held it until 1612, and was in the hands of changing owners until it was bought in 1906 by a young man who was to become the Rev. Father Aelred, and by whose enthusiasm and energy the present handsome wide-eaved monastery was built. Father Aelred, it is said, failed to make the island pay, although he gathered large funds together for the building, and endeavoured to farm it well, and ran a small steam boat to convey visitors at a good fee. He was an Anglican, but changed to the Roman Catholic belief while at Caldey, and so lost the support of his early subscribers. Tales are still told of his liberality, and the freedom he allowed his monks, and some say there was undue laxity. He wandered to America when his little band of Benedictine monks moved from Caldey to Prinknash Abbey, but in his old age he came home to die at Prinknash.

In 1928 the present Trappist (Cistercian Order of the Strict Obedience) community bought the island by a loan from the mother house of Chimay in Belgium, and a party of Belgian monks took possession. They have worked hard, chiefly as farmers, to improve farm production, and pay back the loan from the mother house—and they seem to have succeeded.

Today money flows in to the community during the summer months when thousands of visitors pay their 6d. landing fees, and buy the trinkets, scent, post-cards and pottery sold in the two

monastery shops, at Caldey and at Tenby. The scent is largely
home-produced, from lavender and other herbs grown on the
island. In addition there is a large output of table poultry and
farm produce. With no wages to pay (grumble the Tenby shop-
keepers and farmers) of course the monks make the island pay;
and if a word of criticism is possible from the outsider, the hustle
and bustle to make money does not seem altogether in keeping
with the popular conception of the Trappist Cistercian. But there
is much to be paid for after all: including a completely rebuilt
monastery church, destroyed by fire (and apparently uninsured).

Caldey is really delightful, with its clear air, changing skies,
sandy bays and wild flowers. I have frequently stayed in the off-
season as guest of the monastery, and enjoyed the tranquillity of the
great house and the remote atmosphere of this island which is
dedicated to prayer and peace and honest work. I have shared
the monk's day, rising at 3 a.m. and going to bed at 7 p.m.; and
in the interval attending services in one or other of the three
churches, and tramping the island's vivid shore and bays.

The old priory church stands high upon the hill of Caldey and
has a Norman tower with a blunt leaning spire. The floor of the
little church is paved with beach pebbles and the interior is primitive yet pleasing by its appearance of humble strength. An even
greater age than it possesses is suggested by the fine Ogham
stone against one wall, with its inscription both in Ogham lines
and Latin. Professor Macalister believes that this stone may have
been a pagan monument later Christianised by some evangelist
(Cadwgan?) who chiselled away part of the heathen lines and
put on record his deed:

"And I have fashioned the sign of the Cross upon it. I pray
all who return to the mainland to make fervent prayer for the
soul of me, Catuoconus."

The Ogham lines are supposed to represent an Irish name,
MAGL DOBR, which may be an abbreviation for the "Mael-
Doborchon" of Irish literature, but other scholars find other
names in both inscriptions, and we must leave it at that.

The walls of the twelve-celled priory attached to this church are Norman (twelfth century), built defensively round the cloister-garth, and now topped by modern roofs covering rooms adapted for modern usages.

The village church also may have Norman foundations, its thick western doorway is Norman, and it is situated near the sandy hollow which, as the Life of *St Gildas* suggests, once was a sea inlet and harbour. The legend has it that the waves sometimes swept right into the monastic settlement at highest tides. In the yard of this church the monks when they die are buried, without a coffin, but merely with a canopy to protect the head, beneath the sandy soil in which pine trees flourish.

The third church is attached to the modern monastery. Burnt down a few years ago, it has been entirely reconstructed. Its simple altar, detached from walls, is unusual and the whole interior has dignity and beauty; the high altar of the preceding church was conventional but remarkable for being built of stones from the ruins of other famous abbeys and religious houses of Britain.

The day-visitor, if he be male, is permitted to inspect the monastery; ladies have to be content with visiting the churches, and walking along the north and south coasts. The wooded eastern side of Caldey is an enclosure for the meditation and recreation of the monks. However, there is much more to see than can be enjoyed in one summer day. The accessible coast is very fine, a mixture of red sandstone and limestone with caves and blowholes. There are bathing bays: Sandtop in the west, and the north or landing beach.

Lying to the west of Caldey, and accessible at low tide by a rocky causeway, is the limestone block of St Margaret's Island, about eighteen acres large. It is not part of Caldey and in fact is the property of the Picton Castle estate and leased as a nature reserve to the West Wales Naturalists' Trust. It was gradually reduced in size by the quarrying of its limestone, for which purpose it had, in 1841, some twenty-two people inhabiting four cottages, and its small but fertile pasture was farmed. All quarrying both at St Margaret's and Caldey has now ceased, and only the vertical cuttings of the cliff face and some isolated stone-roofed powder houses or explosive stores remain.

There is the ruin of a cottage on great St Margaret's, and on the peninsula of little St Margaret's is the substantial relic of an ecclesiastical building, the history of which is quite obscure. Its foundation must be very old (coins of Constantine and of Carausius have been found on St Margaret's). More recently it was used as a dwelling by quarrymen. The Rev. Dom Bushell, who owned Caldey 1897–1906, gives a ground plan of this ancient house, showing the probable site of the chapel (with corbels), dormitory and refectory. Today cormorants nest in the roofless structure.

The little island is now a remarkably fine sea-bird sanctuary. When Ray and Willoughby visited it in 1662 they found the nests of sea-birds so thick on the ground that it was difficult to place their feet. Rats have colonised the island, no doubt driving out the burrow-nesting shearwaters and puffins, although a few pairs of puffins regularly nest in the inaccessible crevices of the cliffs, where fair colonies of razorbills, guillemots and the charming kittiwake gulls flourish. The top of the island is covered with a luxuriant growth of grass, mallow and nettles.

The fifty or so pairs of cormorants which have bred since time immemorial on St Margaret's have been studied by members of the W.W.N. Trust with interesting results: marking these birds with numbered leg-rings has shown that a high percentage have been shot in rivers and along the coasts of Wales and south to Brittany and the west Iberian coast during their winter wanderings. So many are shot in fact by zealous fishermen and pot-hunters that it is a matter of wonder that the cormorant, which is an unprotected bird, survives; its habit of continuing to lay (and incubate) eggs throughout the early summer no doubt provides the biological answer. At St Margaret's, where all creatures are protected, the cormorants go freely to and fro; and magnificent they look as they stand like gargoyles in the wind on the top of the quarried stacks and the old buildings.

CHAPTER V

MORE ISLANDS

Six years after the adventure of Caerbwdy, and my first introduction to the home of the patron saint of Wales and to the ancient stones of the sun-god religion, I was farming in a tree-lined Monmouthshire valley. But I had never got wild windswept Pembrokeshire out of my system. I dreamed daily of living on one of her beautiful islands. In 1926 I paid my first visit to the magnificent island of Skomer, the home of seals and thousands of sea-birds. In 1927 I went to live on Skokholm, and dwelt there twelve years, shepherding and watching birds, until war compelled a removal. In 1946 I returned for a brief stay; the West Wales Field Society, of which I was then honorary warden and chairman, occupied Skomer and Skokholm, and its members compiled a book about Skomer, the fruit of a whole summer's field work.

Skomer on that first visit late in May 1926 was purple with acres of bluebells, and red and white with campion covering its abandoned farm fields above jagged great cliffs fluttering with thousands of puffins, razorbills, guillemots and various gulls. Its farmhouse was in repair, occupied by a woman in delicate health and her husband and daughter; but the extensive range of modern farm buildings (dated early in the nineteenth century) were already roofless. The last resident to farm Skomer's 700 acres, Captain Davies, had left thirty years or so before. The island was back to its ancient state—a sanctuary for wild sub-oceanic nature. All day the sea-birds passed and re-passed, and at night it was a bedlam of the noisy nocturnal shearwaters which, nesting in burrows, lay hidden during the hours of light.

Later, acquaintance with two of the aged daughters of Captain Davies of Skomer revealed details of the high farming of his occupation: it was a profitable corn and stock farm. The outer edges of the boundary walls of the cultivated land were overlapped with thick cuts of heather to prevent the rabbits jumping over; seed corn was a remunerative crop, eagerly bought by mainland farmers as soon as it was transhipped; cattle, horses and sheep and rabbits were the livestock exports.

The Davies family lived as yeoman-farmers, and entertained friends who came to shoot pheasants, partridges, woodcock and snipe.

Outside the modern walls of stone and earth which bound the central farmery on Skomer lie much older enclosures, which Laws refers to as the largest collection of hut-circles and enclosures he had ever seen. W. F. Grimes has since mapped these remains, which he dates about the Iron Age. They were doubtless contemporary with those mainland huts and field systems which, except on the cliff edge, have largely been eradicated in subsequent husbandry down the centuries. These relics persisted in the wilder acres of Skomer because (on such historical evidence as we have) since the Iron Age Skomer was only farmed intensively for a brief period through the nineteenth century. At all other times it was as unexploited, save for its natural yield of birds and rabbits and pasturage, as it is today.

Similar hut-circles and field systems on St David's Head survive, and at many sites along the coast, often behind the earth and stone ramparts of the cliff forts or castles (marked as "Raths" on O.S. Maps). In some of these bronze pins or fibulae have been found—dating to the Early Iron Age. On the twenty-acre island of Gateholm there are some 130 hut-circles; Romano–British pottery, coins and flints have been found here. We have already mentioned that Roman coins were found on another Pembrokeshire island about the same size as Gateholm—St Margaret's Island, connected like Gateholm at low tide with other land; these therefore could not have been deposited previous to A.D. 350. For hundreds of years people of various breeds and creeds have dwelt in these coastal huts and earthworks.

Irish gold appears as a metal of some importance during this period, and its fame encouraged trade by sailing boats and currachs between its source in the Wicklow mountains and the coasts of Wales and western England. The stormy wet phase of our climate was over and a warmer sub-boreal phase enabled men to cross the sea freely and to trade. Pembrokeshire again seems to have been a centre or port of call for the west-coast traffic between Spain, Brittany, Cornwall and Ireland and the north-west. Not all the visitors were peaceable traders. Goods and chattels (including women and kine) needed to be protected behind palisades and stone or earth walls.

That Pembrokeshire received newcomers of many different races is clear from the excavations of ancient remains of homes and hearths which show that they were occupied by people who worked variously with flint, iron and bronze. These hut-circles and stone and earth forts survived the Roman occupation of Britain—indeed the huts are the progenitors of the little mud or stone built cottages of the Hebrides and western Ireland at the present time, which hardly seem to be much superior to those low-walled homes of the Iron Age and Romano-British man. One or two of the stone beehive-type dwellings still exist in Pembroke-shire—a good example is under rocky Pencaer near Strumble Head.

How did these people of the hut-circles live? They wore a woven tunic or skirt or kilt, cloak or pull-over, cap, and skin shoes, to protect themselves from cold. The women affected ear-rings and amulets of gold or other metal. They tattooed their skins or painted them with woad. The druidical priests are said to have been attired in blue robes. They cooked, and stored food, in pots. They hunted wild animals, but they did not rely solely on these to provide the main diet; they grew corn, and grazed cattle, goats and sheep.

Since Britain had become an island the larger animals were fewer: bear, beaver and wolf were common (though extinct to-day), and there were bison or wild ox, deer and hares. Rabbits were confined to the Continent—they had not returned since the last warm interglaciated continental period; their absence made possible better grazing conditions on the sunny coastal strips and islands.

Why was Skomer, above all the islands, so intensively occupied? The 240-acre neighbouring island of Skokholm shows no signs of permanent occupation by Iron Age man, although a few flints have been picked up on its surface. As a farmer and naturalist I like to try to reconstruct the scene of Skomer's intensive occupation both from the estimation of the archaeologists and from studying the traces myself; sometimes the farmer and ecologist may help the antiquarian by viewing the scene from his angle, as the aerial photographer has revealed hitherto hidden fields, post-holes, boundaries.

The archaeologists perhaps have neglected the fact that Skomer almost certainly must have been, as it is today, a great breeding ground of sea-birds, making it attractive to human colonists with its opportunities for unlimited bird-meat which could be eaten fresh in the summer or dried and preserved for the winter. Also, in the absence of rabbits, the island would yield a rich pasture, manured by the droppings of sea-birds. The high plateau, swept by salt winds, is particularly healthy and free from cattle pests (mosquitoes, ticks and other marsh-dwelling insects). Wolves and other large predatory mammals could not cross to the island. Skokholm ought to have been a like attraction, but its smaller size and comparative inaccessibility, swept by savage tide-races, no doubt deterred permanent settlers then as these things have done to the present day.

Skomer was more accessible. Across Jack Sound it is only 624 yards to Middleholm and from thence 80 yards across Little Sound to Skomer. Probably in the Iron Age the crossing was shorter; the land has sunk and been washed away much in 2,000 years. Skomer became a settlement for a late Neolithic or Celtic or other westward-living tribe which exploited its rich plateau and cliffs to the uttermost. Here for many years they may have lived in peace. There is evidence that they were well organised, probably under some strong chieftain; when threatened from outside by rival tribes or other invaders they could withdraw their cattle, women and valuables to the walled defensible camp known as South Castle on the Neck, where there is at present a great fallen rampart across the south-westerly isthmus. On the most easterly isthmus still stands a small stone circle where the tribe doubtless carried out the rites and priestly ceremonies of their pagan religion.

Recent research at the Bird Observatory on Skokholm has shown that when rabbits are excluded from the island pasture the more palatable (sheep or red) fescue grasses dominate the herbage, even conquering bracken and heather. Fescue is tolerant of nitrogen; for instance on the rabbit-free island of Grassholm where sea-birds abound, it completely covers the island. There is every probability that Skomer was covered with fescue in the Iron Age, and if so its 700 acres of pasture could have carried probably 100 cattle and 300 primitive sheep all the year round.

In addition, if it yielded in sea-birds the produce which it was estimated to yield in 1946—from 200 thousand adult sea-birds —there would have been a harvest of 100 thousand large eggs; and about 70 thousand young birds which would, roughly, represent about 25 tons of edible bird meat. Perhaps then we should no longer wonder at the evidence of intensive occupation of this bounteous island. It must have been a highly desirable place, easy to defend, rich in grazing and bird-meat, and free of wolves and beasts of prey. (For the last reason of course an island is necessary to burrowing sea-birds, which would not survive the continued presence of wolves, foxes, badgers, polecats, stoats and weasels.) Probably the form of agriculture at Skomer at that time (the Iron Age) differed little from that of the mainland, where similar early field systems survive in certain coast areas of Pembrokeshire, notably north of St David's, where some of the old boundaries are still in use. It resembled the form of agriculture practised by primitive peasants and small-holders through the centuries down to today. The animals were kept in small fields during the winter, treading and dunging there so that the land was ready for crops in the spring, when they would be turned out on the moor and common land to find their own food until late autumn. A hundred cattle and their calves and 300 sheep and their lambs would have enriched the soil, and the only danger would have been from overstocking, as the human and domestic stock multiplied in prosperity. Primitive types of cattle and sheep would be hardier than modern types, and tougher to withstand privation in winter, but overstocking by man and beast would have the effect of causing erosion in winter and the treading-in and destruction of bird-burrows.

Probably the first human settlers began by building shelters for themselves and their animals, gathering the surface stones to make walls (banked by earth). As the stoniest places were about the rock outcrops these were the most convenient places to start the home—having dry ground, shelter from some winds, a view and plenty of building material. The size of the fold was probably determined by the wealth and status of the builder, as well as by the amount of stone handy. The best way to get rid of stones in a pasture was to make them into protective walls; their abundance may have determined the site and thickness of these hedge-walls. Apparent random and abundant building of walls about fields is a characteristic of stony country: in parts of Ireland and Wales some hedge-walls are thick and numerous in order to absorb this abundant stone; those on Skomer are moderately thick, and may not have been very tall.

What were the animals and crops of these early farmers? It has been suggested that it would have been difficult to transport cattle in the primitive canoes of these early peoples, but we do not think this an obstacle. Even today full-grown cows are carried in frail canvas canoes in the West of Ireland, and in any case the settlers could have begun with calves.

Was corn grown? There does not seem to be any other explanation of so many small enclosures, unless they were used for laying up grass for hay. The fact that many of the enclosed fields show positive or negative level steps or "lynchets" is not, however, proof that they were arable and under plough or spade. If animals are kept in a small field for a long time, as when wintering, they will cause the soil to "float" downhill, especially in wet weather, as anyone can see by looking at a farm-gateway, trodden by cattle or other stock, at the foot of a declivity. (The land is then said, in agricultural parlance, to be "poached".) If Skomer was intensively inhabited, as seems likely from the number of enclosures, land would have to be put up for hay for wintering cattle, since no wild hay would have had the chance to grow on the heavily stocked outsummering pastures. But excellent grass and clover hay would be grown in enclosures trodden by cattle in winter; at the same time these fields would be "lynchetted" by the action of treading beasts. As for sheep, these would not require corn or hay, but only a night fold for protection and milking.

Some of the ancient fields on Skomer, especially those close to the remains of dwellings, were stockfolds and some grazing (or summer cropped) fields. All have signs of being surrounded with good stone walls. Outside of some systems and bounding the common land is a bigger structure which appears to be a well-defined bank protecting the enclosures from the outsummering animals on the common or boggy land. But some of the smaller fields along the edge of the cliffs and in the Wick valley are in such exposed positions that it is doubtful if they were meant to be enclosed as pastures. Their walls (hedges) are very low and ill-defined and possibly were never stockproof. Now as this exposed area was probably the best site for the burrowing sea-birds, which like to be in windy sites near the cliff-edge (for convenience of taking off near the sea), I suggest that the primitive inhabitants parcelled out the cliff-lands in strips by marking with low boundary walls of stone and/or earth in order to define the ownership of land occupied by highly edible burrowing sea-birds. The harvest of these might have been irregular; on the other hand it was probably a special autumn or late summer harvest, regulated by the chieftain of Skomer, so that the breeding stock was conserved, and only the helpless young birds taken at the moment when they are fattest just before fledging. (We can vouch for the edibility of these young puffins and shearwaters—they are extremely palatable.) A similar system of ownership of puffin-taking sites used to be, and still is, in use in Iceland and the Faeroes, particularly along the steep cliffs; there the right to take sea-birds in hand-nets is a matter of inherited property and the boundaries are indicated by marks on the tops of the cliffs (stones, etc.).

Mr W. F. Grimes in his article in *Archaeologica Cambrensis*, 1950, refers to stone cairns which he cannot explain for certain—they are too small for human dwellings. In our view these (numbers 1, 2, 3, 11, 13 and possibly 33 and 37) were most likely to have been stone *cletts* or small storehouses for drying bird-flesh, fish and mutton, as in the Faeroes today, and as in St Kilda formerly (where many examples still exist in perfect condition today). These cletts were usually U-shaped, with entrance facing north, slightly excavated in the soil, built around with dry-walling through which the wind could blow, and capped with turf (probably taken from the original excavation) to keep out rain. The roof under the turf was a bridge of stone slabs, from which were hung the split and partly sun-cured sea-birds, and other flesh which it was desired to store for the winter. We have tested clett-dried meat (mutton and puffin) which has been hanging for a year in a Faeroe shed of slatted timber which is the modern equivalent of the St Kildan *clett* or the Scandinavian *skeo* or stone drying-house—and it was delicious. The present size of the ruined cairns on Skomer is about right, allowing for the effects of disintegration and robbing. Most of them are sited in windy places. No. 13 seems the most perfect example, facing north, and its nearness to the stream may have been for convenience of washing and cleaning split-open birds, etc.

To the ecologist who examines the evidence on the spot and has read the highly informative paper by Mr Grimes, it seems likely that the builders of these early field systems first found the island a semi-paradise of food and grazing. They "came, saw and settled". They flourished exceedingly at first, taking the abundant sea-birds in thousands, no doubt at first prodigally and with no thought of conserving the breeding adults; and their domestic grazing stock throve and fattened on the salt- and nitrogen-dressed fescue pasture. Even if the sheltered interior of Skomer was covered with bracken, on the arrival of the settlers, this would quickly be cleared by cutting for bedding and by the treading by farm stock; but the fescue may have already conquered, or kept out, the bracken.

In the security of their productive island the settlers would have lived well, and it is axiomatic that they would have bred well too. As the population multiplied, naturally or by immigration, the land may have been parcelled out more carefully, and a system of conserving the breeding stock of sea-birds introduced (as in the Faroes today). Finally as the island became overstocked with people the sea-birds would dwindle by constant exploitation. Gradually Skomer might have become over-exploited, and less attractive, until the population abandoned it, or were driven from it by the visitation of a more powerful tribe plundering and sacking its community of settlers or their descendants.

How long the first settlement lasted, and how many subsequent re-settlements of Skomer there were, we do not pretend to estimate. We can only suggest that it would be many years, and perhaps decades, before the sea-bird population, especially of the accessible burrowing puffins and shearwaters, would re-build their numbers to the mark of 200 thousand breeding adults (providing 20–30 tons* of young bird-meat each autumn) as is the case today—after being reduced almost to vanishing point by the over-exploitation suggested.

The earliest documents which mention the islands of Skomer and Skokholm are Norman. They show that in 1324 they belonged to the Earl of Pembroke; the value of pasturage on the islands of "Skokholm, Scalmeye (Skomer) and Middleholm" was in that year £2 15s., and the rabbit returns £14 5s. The rabbit, after it was introduced in Britain in early Norman times, was for several centuries reckoned a valuable addition to the human diet, and preserved in warrens and on islands.

The Pipe Roll of Edward III records that carcases and skins of rabbits caught in the islands from Michelmas 1325 to January 30th, 1326, made £13 12s. The expenses were: stipend of 3 ferreters, 12s. 3d.; salt for carcases; thread for rabbit nets; boards, nails and cord for the island boat, 3s. 2d. An interesting glimpse into the values of six hundred years ago. The ferreters lived in a house of some sort which already existed on Skomer and on Skokholm, and were each allowed a couple of rabbits a day and were supplied besides with barley meal and cooking utensils.

As the islands were held by the Earl of Pembroke for the king, there is fortunately a series of detailed ministerial accounts

---

* 200,000 adult sea-birds produce 100,000 eggs, equal to 70,000 fledgelings; allowing for losses this is about twenty-five tons of bird-meat.

extant for the period 1324 to 1472, showing that the rabbiting, pasturage, fisheries and right of ferry ("passagium") all provided revenue for the purse of earl or king. A sum also appears for the farming of the sea-birds, which were taken for food, and their feathers used for stuffing mattress and pillow.

George Owen (1603) describes the custom of taking sea-birds on the small islands which were their "chiefe nurserie" in Pembrokeshire. They were "ripe about midsummer, at which time they flushe [flush = fat and fledged], and are taken being ready to forsake their nestes". This is accurate of some sea-birds, which fly in July. He specially describes

"the Puffine, a bird in all respectes bredd of byrdes of his kinde layeing egges fethered and flieing with other birds in the ayre, and yet is reputed to be fishe, the reason I cannot learne. But if I were so ceremoniouse as to refrayne fleshe at seasons, I should hardely adventure to eate this fowle for fishe, yt is a water fowle lesser than the ducke (mallard) and lardger than the teale, footed and beaked like vnto them and breedeth on the Iland of St Davids and other like places."

The taking of sea-birds for food is as old as man. In Richard Carew's *Survey of Cornwall* (1602), contemporary with George Owen's *Description of Penbrokeshire*, we read that the "Puffyn hatcheth in holes in the Cliffe, whose young ones are thence ferretted out, being exceeding fat, kept salted, and reputed for fish as coming nearest thereto in their taste". Because sea-birds came from the sea, and lived on fish, they were regarded as fish for the purpose of religious occasions when fish took the place of meat in the diet.

Sea-birds and rabbits. Skomer and Skokholm seem to have lain unfarmed down the centuries, after the Dark Age. They were occupied in winter by ferreters, and in summer by herdsmen who also gathered the sea-bird harvest.

The date 1824 on the present buildings of Skomer suggests that a considerable rebuilding took place of the farm which existed in the time of Richard Fenton's *Historical Tour through Pembrokeshire* (1810) when the island is mentioned as the property of

A fisherman from the remote hamlet of Marloes, south-west Pembrokeshire

Charles Philipps of St Brides and "let to a tenant, who resides on it. It consists of a large portion of arable land, and abounds with rabbits, two thousand couple of which are annually killed." Of ancient remains Fenton (who was liberal in his careless general statements) adds, "If any ruins ever existed they cannot at present be traced." Obviously he never set foot on Skomer, or he could not have failed to see the extensive old field systems and hut-circles, whose curious history has nearly filled this chapter.

The more recent history of Skomer, particularly its natural history, is contained in the book *Island of Skomer*, published for the West Wales Field Society by the Staples Press. After the Davies family abandoned Skomer, before 1900, it was never fully farmed again, in spite of attempts by succeeding tenants. Its fields were invaded by burrowing rabbits and sea-birds and wind and salt resistant plants. For a while the trawler-owner J. J. Neale leased it for sporting purposes. Others exploited the rabbits or kept sheep there. Soon after our survey of 1946 it was sold to a wealthy Midland industrialist, then purchased by the West Wales Field Society (now the West Wales Naturalist's Trust) and declared a National Nature Reserve and managed by the Trust under an agreement with the Nature Conservancy.

★   ★   ★   ★   ★

While living at Skokholm we often sailed the eight miles to Grassholm, that lonely green mound in St George's Channel which rises from the same submarine reef of basalt stretching from the Marloes peninsula, through Skomer and Grassholm to the Smalls.

Only 22 acres large, Grassholm is waterless and has never been inhabited for more than a few days by man. The Marloes fishermen in their pulling and sailing boats used to camp there in the fine summers of yesterday. There is a tiny natural rock harbour; their little boats could even be hauled up this rock on to the island by block and tackle. They found lobster and crayfish plentiful; "myriads" of sea-birds provided bait for the pots and food—eggs and flesh—for the camp. In those days the fishing gear was

Cross fashioned by pre-Norman Christian Celts, Carew, south Pembrokeshire

light enough to be carried complete in the boat: a score of hazel-and-twine pots, a trammel net for crayfish which would also entangle puffins if laid along the cliff edge at night, and a box or two and a barrel to store the catch and hold a week's food and drink. Traces of an ancient stone bird-catching corral exist.

The little island called to the fishermen in fine weather, as it has ever called to me. I have slept there, once for a whole week, in making a film of the life of the gannet. There is a deep delight to be out at sea, far from mainland cares in fine midsummer weather, fishing in the lee of its rocky shore or stretching out upon its lush grass, watching the seals which lie out upon the tidal rocks there, watching its sea-birds and the ceaseless movement of the tides.

Grassholm may once have been a hill overlooking the great plain of the Severn swamp when Britain was undivided from Europe. When the Atlantic drowned the surrounding land the sea-birds, deprived of the outer islands of so-called Lyonnesse, moved in to the enisled hills of Grassholm, Skomer, Skokholm and Ramsey. Grassholm at one period of geological time has sunk lower than it is today, on the evidence of the position of its raised beaches and of its lack of soil. Its bare crown, on rising from the sea, again received the seeds of grasses; these, especially the red fescue (*Festuca rubra*), flourished in the salt air, grew up each summer, and died back each winter to form the present soilless haystack about two feet thick above the rock. Then came the puffins: there is no record of their arrival, but in 1890 J. J. Neale estimated that there were over half a million! They so burrowed the haystack that it gradually became a maze of passages. The flimsy grass roofs fell in by weather and weight of birds, and at last the tenements became too exposed for nesting purposes. The puffins began to leave Grassholm in the next thirty years or so, and it was about this time, according to the late tenant from whom I took over Skokholm, that they invaded Skokholm, where in 1927 there were about 20 thousand pairs. Today there are only a few odd pairs nesting at Grassholm, to which the puffins may yet return if the haystack becomes consolidated again. (However, puffins generally are declining in numbers on the British Isles—

66

many hundreds die annually from waste oil discharged by tankers on the high seas.)

Grassholm is more famous for its great flock of solan geese or gannets, which form the only stable large gannetry in England and Wales. Here a happier tale can be told. In the nineteenth century only a few pairs bred there, as old photographs show. These goose-like birds were plundered by fishermen for food and bait, and their eggs were prized by collectors. For centuries, too, gannets were taken at other gannetries. In Scotland, for example, the solan goose was regularly farmed on the Bass Rock in the Firth of Forth, and at Ailsa Craig in the Firth of Clyde. Hector Boethius, writing in 1526, describes the young gannet as being "so extreme fat as that when they eat them they are placed in the middle of the room, so as all may have access about it, their arms stripped up and linen cloaths placed before their cloaths to secure them from being defiled by the fat thereof". I can testify to the succulence of young gannet: I once killed a crippled fledgling, and, out of curiosity, grilled its tender flesh, which proved delicious.

Gannets are protected today (though still eaten in Iceland and the Faeroe Islands, and by special permission at Sula Sgeir in the Outer Hebrides) in the British Isles, and they have increased universally: at Grassholm from twenty nests in 1883 to approaching 15 thousand nests in 1956. At the same time the grey seals, of which only one was noticed in 1890, today form a herd of up to a hundred lying out on the Grassholm rocks at low tide.

*   *   *   *   *

From Grassholm westwards to the loneliest land of Pembrokeshire and the most westerly land of all Wales, the Smalls, is six miles—an hour's fast sail across the tide races and shoals of the Hats and Barrels.

The Smalls, Hats and Barrels have no doubt been known to west coast mariners for many centuries; they appear as a dangerous reef in the early charts. They were however seldom remarked in the early accounts of Pembrokeshire before the project for the building of the lighthouse in 1765 called public attention to their dangers.

Leland (1506) in his *Itinerary in Wales*, describing the Pembrokeshire islands and rocks, noted that:

"Schoukold [Skokholm] Isle yoinith to Scalmey [Skomer] bygger isle then she, onli a passage for shippes deviding them. As I remembre it liyth souther then Scalme. These isles ly not far from the shore in the side of the mouth of Milleford Haven. Beyownd Scalmey farther ynto the ende of the Severn Se lieth a great blakke and hy rokke lyke an isle. Gresse Holme [Grassholm] is a good way into the se, and is but smaulle and without habitation."

Looking, as probably Leland did, at the islands from some height on the Pembrokeshire mainland, it might be possible to see the Smalls as a low black rock on a clear mid-afternoon which is the hour when the lowest spring tides occur in West Wales. Otherwise the only "high black rock" to the west would have been the South Bishop rock, a good deal to the north of the position described by Leland.

George Owen (1552–1613) in his *Description of Penbrokeshire* mentions that "ffarre of in the sea standeth the Iland Gresholme so called of Mr. Saxton, but of the neighbours Walleyes" (the *Gwales in Penvro* of the Mabinogion), but he does not mention the outer rocks.

In 1765 a certain John Phillips of Liverpool set about obtaining a lease from the Treasury of the Smalls rock with the idea of erecting a lighthouse there and profiting from the revenue from the dues. A lease was not granted until 1774. Phillips employed the engineer Henry Whiteside, who with eight miners, a blacksmith and two labourers, sailed from Liverpool in the vessel *Unity* on June 17th, 1775, to begin erecting the lighthouse. In the following three and a half months they were only able to work an aggregate of nine whole days on the main rock. However, in that time they bored a hole eighteen inches deep for the centre pillar, marked out the sites for the other piles, and built a hut. There was space to work above high tide in all but the worst summer gales, and high hopes were entertained of completion by the end of the summer of 1776. After great labour it was finished and on September 1st, 1776, the first Smalls lighthouse exhibited its light—a white one with a "pellucid green" light above it, the latter so screened as to guide mariners between the Barrels and Grassholm, or the Hats and the Smalls: a confusing and dangerous business—and the green light was soon abandoned. It was built with eight flanking pillars, five of wood and three of iron, and a strong centre pedestal. There were two rooms: a living apartment and above it the lantern housing. A rope ladder led from a trapdoor in the floor to the rock below. This curious structure, with frequent repairs and alterations, was to survive for over eighty years, in spite of jocular and caustic comments from those mariners and travellers who viewed it with astonishment as they sailed the St George's Channel. "A strange wooden-legged Malay-looking barracoon of a lighthouse" was one description. Nevertheless many ships' captains were glad of its gleam in bad weather, and recorded their appreciation.

According to Fenton (*Historical Tour through Pembrokeshire*, 1811) Whiteside himself determined to spend the first winter in the new lighthouse. It turned out a violent one—the house on piles groaned and staggered before the gigantic waves and winds of the open Atlantic. By February 1st, 1777, Whiteside was forced to write a letter asking immediate assistance before the next spring tide

"or we fear we shall all perish; our water near all gone, our fire quite gone, and our house in a most melancholy manner. . . . We were distressed in a gale of wind upon the 13th of January, since which we have not been able to keep any light; but we could not have kept any light above sixteen nights longer for want of oil and candles."

This letter was addressed to Thomas Williams Esq., of Tre-lethin, St David's, the agent for the lighthouse, and was put in a corked bottle, and the bottle into a cask on which was painted "Open this and you will find a letter". Three such packets were launched upon the stormy sea. One travelled far and took two months to reach Galway Bay in Western Ireland. The other two came ashore in Pembrokeshire, one actually into the creek under

Trelethin a few days after being consigned. Relief was immediately sent.

In the stormy winter of 1800–1 two keepers were on duty in the improved wooden lighthouse. One was taken ill and died. Failing to attract attention by flying distress signals the surviving keeper was obliged to tear down the wooden bulkhead of the living room to make a coffin for his mate. This coffin with its burden was lashed outside to the gallery rail, where it remained for three months before relief came. After this terrible experience three keepers have always been on duty together at the Smalls lighthouse.

The lighthouse dues became very valuable as shipping increased. Trinity House endeavoured to purchase the lease in 1823, but refused to pay the figure of £148,430 demanded by the lessee, who was now enjoying a comfortable £10,000 a year. In 1836 Trinity House secured the lease for £170,468, based on 16½ years purchase. By 1852 the annual revenue had risen to £22,132.

In 1856 the Board of Trade sanctioned the building of a new lighthouse in stone. This, the present structure, was completed and lit by August 7th, 1861. It cost £50,125, is 126 feet high, and painted with red and white horizontal bands. The group flash of three is visible 17 miles. A lower fixed red light on the east side is so masked as to cover only the dangerous shoals and reefs of the Hats and Barrels, Grassholm, Skomer and Skokholm. Thus, in a better fashion, it followed the purpose of the "pellucid green" light of the first lighthouse.

It was interesting to find that the stumps of the oak pillars of the 1775 structure are still sound, preserved and almost petrified with salt—a tribute to the planning of Phillips, the engineering of Whiteside, and the quality of British oak. Only one stump has disappeared in the interval of twenty-one years between 1934 and 1955, the dates of my visits with a camera to the Smalls.

The strong tide in St George's Channel begins to run southeast at the Smalls about low water Dover, according to the Admiralty Chart. By my observation this south-going stream begins about three and a half hours after local high water (at Milford Haven) and continues for six and a half hours, when there is a brief period of dead or slack water. The stream then runs almost due northwards until three hours after high water, before the next slack water at change of tide. North and south streams are truest direction and at full strength (up to five knots, spring tides) at high and low water. For the two hours each side of both half ebb and half flow the streams are more erratic: they become thrust in an easterly direction towards half flow and westerly towards half ebb. The stream runs fastest around the exposed shoals and rocks near the surface as these impede the mass of moving sea; and violent eddies occur at high and low water.

The mean spring tide is 21 feet. These figures are for the Smalls, and probably fit the Hats and Barrels. Storm-waves sweep the whole of the Smalls rock at high water, so that no plant other than seaweed or marine algae can live. The stone lighthouse itself sways slightly on its solid base (solid for a height of 45 feet), in severe gales, but as each stone is pinned to its neighbour, this movement is regarded as "the healthy elasticity of a living thing".

The *Geological Survey*, 1916, Part XII (The South Wales Coal-field), describes the Smalls, without mentioning the Barrels, as consisting of low islands and half-tide rocks, made up of basalt, and on the extreme south, of a dolerite very like that of Pigstone Bay in Skomer Island. The strike of rocks on Grassholm and the Smalls is Caledonian, nearly north-east and south-west (hence the harbours or sea-creeks in both all run in these directions), whereas at Skomer and the nearby mainland the strike is Armorican, east–west.

Heavy seas break over the Hats in bad weather, but no rock was visible at low tide during the calm weather of our summer visits. The laminaria covering the highest underwater rock barely touched the surface of the sea, and our boat *Mayflower* could pass over the top of each reef without danger, even at dead low water. At this state of tide the strong current running southwards caused innumerable whirlpools and eddies due to the underlying reeds and *Mayflower* behaved erratically as she moved slowly eastwards above and across the inaccessible Hats in the direction of the black knob of the Barrels.

At dead low water on July 7th, 1955, a very brief landing

was made on the Barrels—apparently for the first time in history, but as there was a considerable tide wash I could not remain long enough to collect geological specimens. This was done seventeen days later, on July 24th, when Peter Davis and Michael Odlum went ashore (again a scramble at a favourable moment) while I remained at hand keeping the dinghy clear of the tideswell.

The strong south-going stream pours down past the one rock which dries up to 10 feet at springs, so that the only convenient approach is from the south within the eddy caused by the Barrels Rock itself.

The Barrels at low tide has an uneven dromedary-shaped surface, with deeper water on the south side close to the westerly extremity. Here the landing was made, upon the *pelvetia* seaweed zone. The whole rock is approximately 25 yards east to west, with a maximum of 6 yards (east block) north to south. There is a central strike or depression running north-east, south-west, as at Grassholm and the Smalls, through which the rising tide quickly washes (as we found on both visits). The larger east block is higher by some 3 feet than the lower west portion, and shoals away more on its south side making a landing alongside more difficult.

Some 15 lb. of rock was cut from the surface with a cold chisel. Specimens were sent to the Geological Survey Museum. The rock proves, as was not unexpected, to be of the same volcanic series as the Smalls, Grassholm and Skomer.

Attached to the surface of the rock specimens from the Barrels were the following marine algae, kindly identified by Mr A. E. Wade of the National Museum of Wales, who gives the following list:

Pelvetia canaliculata (a tiny fragment)
Cruoria pellita, the purplish-black encrustation
Corallina officinalis. The pinkish and white encrustation is the basal thallus of this species.

In addition we collected by hand (July 7th):

Thong Weed, *Himanthalia lorea*
Oar-weed, *Laminaria digitata*

72

There were also attached to the rock numbers of rather small common mussels, *Mytilus edulis*, the barnacle *Balanus balanoides*, the limpet, *Patella* sp., but apparently no periwinkles, *Littorina*.

During fishing operations while *Mayflower* lay in the eddy a few score yards from the Barrels, we took mackerel *Scomber scomber*, and pollack, *Gadus Pollachius*; and a large blenny or eel-like fish (not a garfish), which was later fried and found delicious and eaten before it was properly identified! A tope shark 5 feet long attacked the pollack as we drew them in on the 24th.

Pollack were also freely taken in the channels between the Smalls rocks, in spite of some hundred seals present.

A basking shark about 10 feet long was seen near the Hats on the 7th, lazily sunning at the surface with fin protruding.

Porpoises, *Phocaena phocaena*, were seen during the crossing between Grassholm and the Smalls, and two common dolphins, *Delphinus delphis*, rose sportively around *Mayflower* on July 7th.

We were well aware that the Smalls reef is a lying-out ground of the Atlantic Grey Seal, *Halichoerus grypus*. Records kept by lighthouse keepers for me in 1947-9 show that up to 150 were present during the months April to September, but only a few individuals were noticed in winter. It is impossible for this seal (which unlike the common seal, *Phoca vitulina*, requires ground above high tide on which to nurse its calf for the short two or three weeks of lactation) to calve in safety at the Smalls and still less at the Barrels.

On both July 7th and 24th between eighty and a hundred grey seals were counted lying out on the reefs to the south of the Smalls lighthouse. Some of these rolled into the sea on our approach, but the more distant individuals remained at their basking posts. Those in the water showed little fear, and swam within a few yards of *Mayflower*. They are of course completely unmolested by man in this wild spot. At a rough estimate some forty per cent appeared to be fully adult bulls, forty per cent mature cows, and the rest immatures between one and three years old.

No seals were seen over the Hats reef—there is nowhere for them to lie out in this presumably excellent fishing ground.

At the Barrels one yearling seal was asleep on the rock on our approach on July 7th, and on the 24th two older seals (about two years old) were disturbed from their afternoon siesta. On both these dates about forty to sixty seals were present at Grassholm. It seems obvious that the whole chain of islets and outlying rocks, including the Smalls, off the Pembrokeshire coast is within the territory or range of the same herd of probably one thousand grey seals of all ages with breeding beaches and caves at Skomer, Ramsey and along the mainland of south-west Wales.

A detailed report of this first landing on the Barrels Rock appeared in *Nature in Wales*, Summer issue 1956.

CHAPTER VI

THE WEST COAST

LIKE a splendid spider the borough of Haverfordwest and its road system dominate the west coast, itself dominated by the perfect arc of St Bride's Bay. One of the two or three good inns at Haverfordwest makes a convenient base for the exploration of the west coast.

Built around its great castle upon a hill, Haverfordwest is a town with charm, and worth a little quiet exploration. Its position at the salt head of the Western Cleddau river, navigable for small cargo ships to the town quay at high tide, and its central position have resulted in it becoming the administrative centre for the county, although Pembroke remains nominally the capital.

The castle was probably built by Gilbert, Earl of Clare and Pembroke, who died round about 1115. It stood guard over the walled town at its foot along the riverside. Haverfordwest was made a borough by charter in the reign of Henry III. We hear of its being burnt in 1219 by Llewellin the Great, and in 1405 Owain Glyndwr laid unsuccessful siege to the castle and his French allies sacked the town on this occasion.

Haverfordwest saw little more of battles save during the Civil War, when the Castle was taken from the Royalists by Parliamentary troops in 1645. Its vicissitudes have been those of a peaceful agricultural town, enjoying the trade by land which came from the Welsh in the north, and the trade which came, often by sea, through the enterprise of the Flemish and English of Little England beyond Wales. Pestilence struck grievously with the Black Death. In 1544 Haverfordwest was classed as a decayed town.

Ship-building along the tidal water south of the town flourished up to 1853, but the coming of the railway and of steam navigation were signals of its decline as a port. Nowadays it is a rare event if a sea-going merchant vessel berths at the old quay at spring tide.

About 1200 Robert de Hwlfordd founded a Priory of Black (Austin) Canons close to the town: the remains of this once-vast monastery can be seen by following the west bank of the river towards Haroldstone, the birthplace of a favourite of Queen Elizabeth I, Sir John Perrott, Lord Deputy of Ireland, whom however she eventually cast into the Tower of London, where he died in 1592.

Sir John, it is said, was the natural son of Henry VIII by Mary Berkeley, a lady of the court, although his legal father was Sir Thomas Perrott, gentleman of the bedchamber, of Jestynton (Eastington, near Angle) and Haroldstone. In appearance he was much like the King, and had the same unbridled courage and temper, which got him into constant trouble.

The three churches of St Mary's, St Thomas's and St Martin's deserve careful survey; St Mary's is probably the finest in the county (next to the cathedral) with its fifteenth-century panel roof above the chancel, and arches, two centuries older, bearing grotesque carvings, and numerous memorials.

Haverfordwest itself has changed little in a hundred years, but its suburbs have spread rapidly since the end of World War II, due largely to the building of rural industry factories, the growth of local agricultural productivity, and the establishment of W.D. bases in the county. Its population is now about 8 thousand, and with Milford Haven (12 thousand) forms a busy populous centre in the heart of the county, with good main roads between and to Fishguard, Carmarthen, Tenby and Pembroke.

Just as Pembroke people go to the Freshwater Bays for their seaside relaxation, Haverfordwest dwellers (known locally as "Harfats") seek out the lovely sandy Broad and Little Havens, half a dozen miles to the west, on the great sickle curve of St Bride's Bay.

This west coast served by and serving Haverfordwest begins at St Ann's Head, following a wild rock-bound coast to Marloes Sands, where fine seas often make surfing possible. It is well worth walking north-west to the most westerly point of the Land's End of Wales here, to the Deer Park, overlooking Jack Sound, where spring tides roar through at the rate of 5 knots

at high and low water. The cliff path is of course part of the Pembrokeshire Coast National Park, although it is not yet everywhere
made easy to the foot. Just here it is possible to cross at low tide
to the little island of Gateholm, notable for its settlement of
Romano-British hut circles. The Deer Park itself now has no
deer, but is bounded by the great defensive fosse or embankment
—two thousand years old—of an Iron Age camp.

From the Deer Park the rocky basalt coast continues past the
unspoilt inlet of Martinshaven, a remote haven and beach for
small fishing boats, and ferry for the islands of Skomer and Skokholm. (Permission to land on these islands must be obtained
beforehand—the local Marloes boatmen will advise on this.)
Marloes, formerly a lobster-fishing village of some consequence,
lies inland on the whaleback of the western peninsula, and not
long ago enjoyed a notoriety with Llangwm for its hostility
to strangers. But nowadays the summer visitor has become almost
a cottage industry, with food and accommodation provided at
moderate prices, and boats to go fishing or to the islands. The
sturdy Marloese, with their bold, fair Flemish-type faces and
frames, are an independent people; their strong local dialect has
a pleasing lilt to most ears.

The cliff path from Martinshaven to Musselwick Sands follows
a prickly path through gorse where stonechats flit and click,
and—be it noted—adders bask on sunny days. Musselwick is safe
bathing at low tide, but is best avoided when high tides sweep
to the walls of the black cliff.

The walk along the rich red cliffs to the Tower Rocks is very
pleasant, with magnificent views of St Bride's Bay. Fulmar
petrels have settled to breed on sheer red walls above a translucent
blue sea.

Near the Towers is yet another *Rath*, or British peninsular
camp with earthen defences in depth. At the Nab itself is the
site of a flint chipping factory or "floor" dating about 5000 B.C.
Students have scraped and turned much of the surface in search
of worked flint tools and flakes.

Pass down by the field walls near the 200-year-old residence
of Hill or St Bride's Castle (now known as Kensington Hospital

for tubercular children), to charming, often deserted St Bride's Haven, fit only for a bathe or a boat in fine weather, for the swell and the sea in some winds are treacherous here.

In the distance are the St Bride's Stacks, small rocky islets, the home of cormorant, gull and grey seal. These can be reached by boat from Martinshaven, St Bride's Haven or Little Haven. The cliff path from St Bride's Haven to opposite the Stacks is again along red cliffs full of sea-birds, with buzzard and peregrine falcon, and often the rare chough is recorded by the watchful eye. Seals swim in the surf below, and in autumn may calve down in the almost inaccessible cliff caves and beaches.

So by an elevated cliff-edge path proceed by Gouldtrop Roads (past the abandoned sailing lifeboat station) to the popular Little and Broad Havens.

Northwards are the Druidston Chins—again fine cliffs (now no longer sandstone, for we are on the spent coal-measure strata) with caves and sandy beaches below. Nolton Haven is a curious gorge in these cliffs where the road comes down to sea-level. Soon the three-mile-long beach of Newgale Sands begins to open, where even in the calmest offshore breezes the surf rolls majestically. By this grand shore caravans and summer shacks have accumulated, but the sands are so immense that the disfigurement seems small—or perhaps one is so drawn to gaze seawards that the inland view is unimportant. Good surfing and sand yachting are possible, although the sea never seems so warm here as in shallow Saundersfoot Bay.

After heavy storms at low tide the stumps and debris of a great forest are occasionally unveiled along the Newgale shore.

Back of Newgale lies the broad wild duck and snipe haunted morass of the Landsker, the dividing line between the English and the Welsh peoples, with Roche Castle solitary and watchful on the southward height. Northward we are in the Welshery, in a wilder land of steeper hills and deeper bogs, of rocks and less fertile soil, and high windy furze-grown cliffs rich in sea-birds, buzzards, herons, falcons and choughs.

Solva is the only village of consequence before St David's is reached, and lies in two parts. Lower Solva rests at the head of the deep tidal harbour or drowned valley of the stream, which meanders seaward after its agreeable journey through a bare sunlit glen full of primroses, foxgloves and kingcups in spring. There is a woollen mill here—or was at the time I wrote this— where you may buy the warm homespun Welsh wool blanket at very modest prices, known as Middle Mill.

Upper Solva is on the hill above, and gazes upon the narrow entrance to the harbour, and upon the whaleback of the "Gribin", a curious tongue of land dividing the valley, which, now the property of the National Trust, is covered with early British earth works and defensible mounds. Solva once had a couple of dozen sailing ketches and schooners registered in her port, which carried away the corn and brought back coal and anthracite, until modern steamships and road transport quite killed this local trade. Solva is a most attractive place for a holiday, especially for those who like boating, fishing and walking. Much of the cliff land outside the farm fields is owned by, or covenanted to, the National Trust.

To the north-west, along the Trust land, where furze is a golden glow in spring, we come to Caerbwdy, where this book began.

*　　*　　*　　*　　*

Ramsey Island terminates the northern horn of St Bride's Bay. The name may be Norse, perhaps a corruption of Hrafn's Ey, Island of the Raven.

The island—600 acres—stands proudly like a Viking ship, riding at anchor in the savage ride-races off St David's Head, its twin hills grey and yellow in winter, green and red in summer. This magnificent island was a landmark for shipping going coastwise from the Severn towards north Wales, and before the days of lighthouses the island's high hills must have been the first glimpse of Wales for sailing craft coming east from southern Ireland and along the ancient trade route from the Mediterranean. One is not surprised to find that two chapels or cells were built on the island, one by the Breton Justinian (supposedly about 500 A.D.) and one (according to Fenton) as early as 186 by Tyfanus or Devanus or Devynog, who must therefore have been one of the first Christians to preach in Wales; he was sent to Britain by Eleutherius, and is said to have retired to Ramsey to end his days in peace. A heap of stones in the little valley by the present farmhouse is pointed out as the site of his cell.

The chapel of St Justinian on Ramsey was already three-quarters fallen into the sea when the late L. D. Whitehead, owner of the island, showed me what he believed to be the foundations of this early Christian cell: it then lay on the edge of the crumbling verge of the eastern cliffs north of the farm buildings. Whether Devanus, or Justinian, or both, ever lived on Ramsey will probably never be proved. But we know that this St David's peninsula and its islands was the hub of a considerable sea-trade and it would have been easy for an evangelical priest to reach Wales by way of St David's in the early centuries A.D.

The traditions and tales of the lives of the saints are numerous; they come from the hagiological literature. One story I heard while staying on Ramsey was that a land bridge formerly connected the island with St David's. But being troubled by many visitors wishing to do him honour Saint Justinian prayed that the bridge might disappear. The prayer was granted; as if chopped down by a giant axe, the land bridge now exists only as the Bitches, a series of submerged or tidal rocks through which the tide runs with great violence at high water. The great rock closest to the island, the bastion of the bridge, known as the Great Bitch, seems as if cloven asunder, and through this "Axe-Cut" pours the north-going rising tide.

When I first landed on Ramsey this flood water dashed through the slate ravine and foamed across the mouth of the little cove which served as a harbour beneath the farmhouse. Our boat was tossed through this race willy-nilly—as we had not realised its danger until it was too late to turn round.

There were then farming the island a widow and her two sons, none of them competent by sea or on the land. They had just lost their boat, one son had been gored by a bull, and two horses and some sheep had been killed by lightning. The island swarmed with rats and rabbits, and strangely there was one lone escaped golden eagle preying on this swarm. The Lewis men, forgetting

Salmon-fishermen in their primitive coracles assist at the sheep-washing at Cenarth, on the river Teify

this good service, wanted to shoot this magnificent stray bird because of its alleged predation of lambs. The eagle had escaped from Skomer Island, had drifted north and pitched appropriately on Ramsey's higher hills.

Subsequently an attempt was made to provide this eagle with a mate. Captain Knight (owner of "Mr Ramshaw", the tame eagle) delivered a splendid female golden eagle to Ramsey. The resident eagle at once attacked the newcomer, and drove it from the island. She was washed up drowned soon after. The lone monarch reigned a few more years until Lewis senior shot it one spring, during the lambing season. It proved to be a female—hence the disagreement.

The Lewis family gave up Ramsey. My friend, Whitehead, industrialist and countryman, bought it, intending to restore the farm, now in a derelict condition. First he plugged the Axe-Cut with hundreds of tons of concrete, to divert the boisterous tide-race from the harbour-entrance and form a quay. Then he mended or rebuilt the house and farm buildings. The mason in charge of the repairs and the dam-building, Bert Griffiths, was so taken with life on the island that he settled down as Whitehead's tenant, and farmed the land with skill.

Ramsey makes an excellent farm if you can stand the exposure. It is dry and sunny, good for seed corn, healthy for cattle and sheep. Courageous men have made money there, using combine harvesters and flying herds of sheep and kine. In 1954 the rabbits nearly all died out from myxomatosis.

It was of old part of the income of the bishops of St David's, in 1326 rented for 2d. an acre per year, and it would hold 10 horses, 100 large cattle and 300 sheep, "and the pasture for each head of great cattle is worth 2d., and for every sheep 2d., and they say that the lord [Bishop] is able to take thence 100 loads of rushes and heath; each load is worth 3d., and the Lord is able to take there, without injury to the stock, 500 rabbits for cooking, and they are in actual value worth 33s. 4d.". For the right to ferry to and from the island, the ferryman had to pay to the bishop two fowls, at Christmas.

Most visitors to Ramsey go by local boat from the lifeboat

6

Cave on Caldey Island—in many such caves prehistoric remains are numerous station at Porth Stinian, which lies under the well-preserved though roofless chapel of St Justinian in the grounds of the White-head's mainland base. A small landing fee is payable, but many do not land if the weather is calm, for then it is worth staying in the boat for the "round Ramsey" sea-trip. The rock-bound coast has probably forty caves, in many of which seals will be seen, especially in September and October when the Atlantic Grey seal drops its calf on the island cave beaches. The west face of Ramsey is wild with high cliffs, inlets, bays and islands where great numbers of sea-birds breed: guillemots, razorbills, various gulls, including kittiwakes, oystercatchers and fulmar petrels. Here is the eyrie of the peregrine falcons which were better than the Norway goshawks of Henry II, who tested them on his way to Ireland. Here too can be seen the rare red-billed crow or chough, and ravens and buzzards, and even herons nesting in the cliffs.

Southward is Ynys Bery, a high stony ridged island which I once explored in vain in search of storm petrels, but found only purple sheets of the lovely tufted vetch. Westwards are the Bishops and Clerks, little islands and rocks dedicated to the seals and sea-birds, except the southernmost, the South Bishop, on which Trinity House built the present roomy lighthouse. From the South Bishop light on a clear night the flash of the nearest Irish lighthouse—Tuskar—is visible.

We now know that the young seals born on Ramsey's open beaches and cave-beaches may travel across the fifty miles of St. George's Channel. We have marked these seals with numbered metal rings (around the hind toe) in order to study their migrations; some have been recovered at the Saltee Islands, in sight of Tuskar, off the coast of Wexford, and others along the south coast of Ireland. Some have gone south to Cornwall and at least two have swum to Brittany. Most of these recoveries are of young seals, which apparently wander most during the first few months of their lives—as many other animals are known to do.

Barely a quarter of a century ago the local lobster fishermen were the enemies of the seals, which they shot when adult, or slaughtered as white calves helpless upon the beach. But today the inshore fishermen find it more profitable to take visitors out in their boats to see the seals, and they no longer molest these, the largest of land-breeding British wild mammals. As a result Ramsey's seals have become semi-tame, and one may watch the bolder matrons suckling their single calf without taking alarm at the appearance of the human watcher.

Seals are protected by law over the four months, September–December inclusive, during which they are breeding. The cow comes to land to drop her calf above the high water line upon some remote beach. Her milk is very rich (50 per cent fat). The calf gains weight at the rate of about 3 lb. a day, whereas the dam, who does not feed herself during the lactating period, loses an average of 6 lb. a day. At 14–21 days the cow's milk dries up and she mates with the bull. The calf retreats to the back of the cave or beach and completes its moult from the white natal pelt to the first mottled or spotted coat (black upon grey and brown background) resembling the colours of the adult. Thus after a lactation period of the same length as that of the mouse, the young seal is weaned. At this age it is fat and may weigh a full hundredweight, or more than twice its weight at birth.

The role of the bull seal at this season is to patrol the water outside a nursery beach or cave, and keep to himself the cows using that beach. He drives away rival aspirants to the harem, but after mating a succession of cows using the nursery he may be spent, and in weakness forced to give way to a vigorous fighting new bull. Except when breeding bull seals are not quarrelsome, however, and may be seen at other seasons lying out together on basking rocks, or even playing in the sea like care-free children. The adult bull is distinguishable by his large head with its Roman profile and prominent widely spaced nostrils; he is usually, but by no means always, much darker than the cow and has a thick neck with heavy wrinkles of hide. The cow has smaller features and a more slender neck, is often a light grey with thrush-like streaky markings. Black cows are rare, but I have seen a few. The adult pelt of this seal is covered with hair and of no value commercially as fur. As it dries in the sun it appears to change colour from grey to near-white, as the hair fluffs open.

CHAPTER VII

THE NORTH COAST

No piece of coast in Wales is quite so lovely in its romantic and wild unspoilt appearance as the north shore of Pembrokeshire, of which St David's Head, nearly if not quite the noblest prospect of all, has already been described. My walk there was one of great beauty, passing over the old Pilgrim's Way, the furze-grown track of Ffos y Mynydd, at the back of Penberry Rock, where primroses and the lovely blue vernal squill were in flower.

There is no town or even village of any size between St David's and Fishguard. Only colour-washed farmhouses, clustering at certain points, give the impression of villages; they have such Welsh names as Croesgoch (the Red Cross), Trevine, Porthgain, Abercastell and Mathry.

The land is hilly, often wet with rushes and full of stones. The natives are altogether a tougher race than in the south, hard-working Welsh peasants, living by the pure and admirable economy of producing most of their own food from the stony soil, paying few wages, handling and saving money sparingly, bartering goods and exchanging labour with neighbours. This independence and ability to exist on poor land yet makes for courtesy and a pleasing hospitality towards the infrequent visitor who knocks upon the door of the remote coast farmhouse in search of advice or perhaps permission to trespass.

Trevine was once the dwelling place of Bishop Tully (1460–82), but nothing remains of his "palace". At Abercastell a hundred years ago smuggling is said to have been extensive during the brisk coastwise trade conducted in wooden ketches and sloops, carrying corn, limestone and anthracite. Porthgain was noted for its slate quarries, now gaunt and unused.

Mathry is a perfect example of a medieval hill-top village, probably on the site of an early British one. All roads seem to converge there, where the fine view covers Pembrokeshire west of the Prescelly mountains. It had a market and a fair, and its church was a land-mark for the wooden ships which once plentifully sprinkled the coast in good weather. It is still the seat of the local magistrates' court.

Its churchyard has a round wall, possibly following the lines of a pagan stone circle. The word Mathry signifies martyr; the church is dedicated to the Seven Saints, said to have been the seven children born on one day to a Pembrokeshire woman whose husband, unable to support them, determined to drown them. He took them to the river Taf, but they were saved by St Teilo who promised to bring them up in the church. For their daily sustenance they had each a large fish which appeared miraculously by the water's edge—hence the name of Dyfrwyr (Watermen) by which they were known. They came to live in Mathry, where in 1720 their stone coffins were said to be still visible in the churchyard. Two gravestones with incised crosses can still be seen in the walls thereof.

There are many stone relics of an earlier age in Dewisland, notably the cromlech of Carreg Samson in the lane of Longhouse Farm. A fine pig was lying asleep under the capstone when I passed that way. On Garn Fawr Rocks towards Strumble Head, there is an unusually complete British settlement with hut-circles; there is a bee-hive stone hut below; and two cromlechs can be seen in St Nicholas parish to the south. Castell Mawr, below Garn Fawr, is a huge rock peninsulated by the sea—it is an Iron Age site too—with the usual defensive ramparts across the narrow isthmus; it faces the tall undulating cliffs of Pwll Deri on which cormorants, fulmars and other sea-birds nest. Atlantic seals are always present in the caves and near the little pebble beaches of this wild and beautiful bay. A new youth hostel lies above it.

By the road above these cliffs is the whitewashed farm of Tref Asser, the reputed home of Bishop Asser, the twelfth century chronicler of the court of King Alfred. The rocky Pencaer peninsula is guarded on the north-west by Strumble Head Lighthouse, flashing its light across St George's Channel towards the Tuskar Light in Ireland, which is but fifty miles distant.

Pencaer was the site of the last invasion of Britain, in 1797, a very curious affair which has been often glamorously misreported. It is accurately described and minuted in a book by Commander E. H. Stuart-Jones, R.N.: *The Last Invasion of Britain*.

Traditional popular accounts describe how a handful of peasant-women of Pencaer, on the landing of the French troops, marched and re-marched past a gap in the rocky heights wearing their red shawls and carrying broomsticks and other long-handled domestic utensils, thus giving the impression of a fully equipped army massing on the heights above. The enemy, expecting a deadly ambuscade, were, it is said, terrified into an easy surrender, more especially as their own ships had fled from the coast.

Commander Stuart-Jones goes back to the root cause of the French invasion, which was inspired by French hatred of England following the bitter wars of the eighteenth century and in particular the hatred of Lazare Hoche, a young general of the Republic who was already famous for having driven into the sea the French Royalists who, equipped and provisioned from English and Channel Island sources, had made an abortive landing at Quiberon in 1795. Into Hoche's hands had fallen the immense booty of stores landed at Quiberon—four thousand cartloads, including thousands of British uniforms and rifles.

Hoche used this windfall in carrying out his particular design of revenge: to invade Britain with twelve hundred convicts (army deserters chiefly) dressed in British uniforms and commanded by an undesirable French subject. The object was to carry out a *chouannerie* in Britain, that is, to foment a revolution, encourage the poor to rise against the crown, and spread terror and civil war. They were to be allowed to loot and filibuster and eventually, if they could, return with all available booty; after which, they were told, they would be allowed to enjoy it in peace under the tropical skies of the French island of St Domingo.

As it turned out an American named Tate, with the same hatred of the English, was put in charge of the buccaneers by Hoche, who issued minute instructions as to the *destruction by fire of the city of Bristol*.

On the 18th February, 1797, the frigates *Vengeance* and *Resistance* set out from Camaret in Brittany before a strong east breeze. Off Land's End Tate hoisted the Russian flag, in passing through a British convoy, to avoid suspicion. On his progress up the Bristol Channel he was obliged to overhaul and sink small craft which would have reported his presence. From these he collected pilots to guide him. But the east wind held and it was impossible to make Bristol.

The alternative was the coast of Wales, off which the squadron was seen on Wednesday, 22nd February, by observers at St David's. By 2 a.m. on Thursday, the expedition had landed unopposed, in perfect weather, at Carreg Wastad Point, close to Fishguard. The local people were slow to realise that this was a genuine invasion, but when the pirates began to loot the farmhouses, the peasants hastily evacuated the immediate parishes, their loaded carts rumbling inland.

The two frigates now departed, by agreement leaving Tate ashore to handle the invasion troops, which were in British uniforms dyed brown. The ships did not desert the troops as commonly reported—it had always been planned they should sail for France at once, and Tate signed a *procès-verbal*, giving the commodore his receipt for safe delivery of the invasion. However, the departure of the ships may have worsened the morale of the piratical ex-convicts. These men were desperately hungry after being deliberately put on a light diet during the voyage; and they tore at the food they found in the farmhouses.

As each house was said to contain a barrel or two from a recent wreck of a wine-carrying ship, the invaders could wash down their Welsh bread, bacon and poultry with a drink best suited to their taste. A few hundred of them became drunk and deserted the camp that night.

The alarm was running through Pembrokeshire and local troops began to muster. Fortunately Tate's army of 1,200 men was making a leisurely day of it in fine weather, and did not at once advance. Thomas Knox, a colonel in command of the local home guard, the Fishguard Fencibles, being roused by one of his men from attending a dance at Tregwynt, a country house not far from Pencaer, went to reconnoitre that peninsula. He did not go down close to the cliffs opposite which the French ships were to be seen with their sails furled, or he would have witnessed the landing. Instead, apparently not fully believing in the invasion, he proceeded to Fishguard, meeting on Goodwick Sands seventy of his Fencibles under Ensign Bowen already moving to repel the French. These stalwarts grumbled when he bade them retreat to their Fort at Lower Fishguard and await reinforcements. Knox's over-prudent action cost him dear: it is possible that had seventy enthusiastic men attacked the landing party immediately they might have contained it from the superior position available on the high cliffs, until reinforcements arrived. Carreg Wastad was one of the worst landing sites for any invasion army on this coast and cost the French vast labour in hoisting up guns, ammunition and stores. Had they boldly landed on Goodwick Sands they could have taken Fishguard by surprise.

Retreat was too much in Knox's mind. He collected more men, and still without contact with the enemy, he began next day to fall back upon Haverfordwest. He sent an order to the bombardiers of the tiny Fishguard Fort to spike the guns and join him; but they were no cowards and refused.

Meanwhile immediately on hearing of the invasion, Lord Cawdor of Stackpole had drawn his Castlemartin Yeomanry from a funeral which this unit was attending in the south of the county, and marched north to meet the enemy, gathering all able-bodied men he could find *en route*. Encountering Knox and his retreating Fencibles he peremptorily required them to fall in and advance.

Cawdor (Squire Campbell) was popular, young and ardent, and a model landowner; and to him must go the credit for the decisive action which followed.

Tate had been told by Hoche that the Welsh people would flock to the French standard and join in the revolution. But his ex-convicts were behaving so badly that wild rumours of their conduct were already spreading through the countryside and alienating any sympathy they might have gained through a friendly approach. Instead of an alliance Tate was greeted with a hostile peasantry who, even before the arrival of Lord Cawdor, were resisting the advance of the French scouts. Whiteside, the engineer who was responsible for building the Smalls lighthouse, had arrived from Solva with a small party of seamen and boldly attacked the Frenchmen, killing one, and wounding and putting to flight others. Prisoners were taken by other Welshmen, but one or two Welshmen lost their lives in trying to drive French soldiers from their fields and farms. One Jemima Nicholas, a cobbler woman of Fishguard, is famous for having, it is reported, gone forth with a pitchfork and captured several Frenchmen and brought them in as prisoners.

With less than six hundred men against double the number of the enemy, Lord Cawdor, on arrival at Fishguard at 5 p.m. on the Thursday, decided to attack the French, whose outposts were now deployed on the heights above Goodwick Sands. The night being very dark, however, the attack was delayed until morning. The English drums beating for the recall were mistaken by the French as sounding the advance, and the French officer ordered his men to retreat, firing as they went. So in the dark the troops marched away from each other in this curious local war, and slept peacefully at a decent distance apart! Both sides were, like children, tired out with the day's events, the Pembrokeshire men with so much marching, the French with landing and looting.

Now came a further anti-climax. The French from the heights of Pencaer had seen the blue coats of Lord Cawdor's men approaching from the south by the turnpike road: but these numbered under six hundred, whereas in a testimony in the French archives it is stated by the French officers that Cawdor was approaching "with troops of the line to the number of several thousand". The historian Stuart-Jones considers that this declaration lends colour to the well-known tradition that it was the Welsh women, arrayed in their red cloaks, who, by gathering as spectators (and even ready to take a part as amateur soldiers), deceived the French into believing that the country had risen *en masse*. Tate, on seeing this army of blue and red, decided to surrender, but on honourable terms which would include the return of his forces to France at the expense of the British

Exchequer. That evening he sent his truce officers to parly with Cawdor at Fishguard, with a brief message of his "desire of entering into a Negociation upon Principles of Humanity for a surrender."

Cawdor demanded unconditional surrender, although he had still not yet half the number of Tate's troops available for the impending battle. Tate reluctantly gave in, and at mid-day what was left of his ex-convicts marched down and stacked arms on Goodwick Sands. All around on the eastward hills and ridges stood the Pembrokeshire yeomen in their blue uniforms, together—we are to suppose—with thousands of Welsh women in their red flannel cloaks (these having been ordered, it is said by several writers, by Lord Cawdor to assemble with stakes, pokers, and household and farm weapons). The impression was of a formidable army ready to attack.

Before dark of this the second day rations of bread and cheese were doled out, and the enemy were marched away to captivity in Haverfordwest castle, jail and church—a ten-hour tramp through the night.

In trying to vindicate his honour in the months and years following, Colonel Knox, accused by his enemies of having retreated dishonourably, felt obliged to challenge Lord Cawdor, who had refused to serve under him in future, to a duel. The site arranged was on a country road near Neyland, but it was never fought—apparently on meeting the duellists and their seconds must have agreed on a satisfaction of honour by words.

*　　*　　*　　*　　*

Fishguard or Goodwick Bay at the time of the French invasion was an open beach haunted by wild geese and ducks in winter, at which season it was unsafe for shipping in a northerly gale, although ships coming south down the Welsh coast found good shelter there in southerly and westerly winds. The harbour at that time was Lower Fishguard, a tidal inlet with a breakwater and wharf, built by Samuel Fenton, which could accommodate a good many small craft at high tide : at low water it is dry.

In 1908 the present breakwater was built from the cliffs of

Goodwick to make the modern Fishguard Harbour. From here the British Railway and Irish boats sail nightly to Rosslare, Waterford or Cork. The crossing is only a few hours by these steamers, which are extremely comfortable. Trains wait at Rosslare to convey passengers to Dublin, Cork, etc.

It is the boast of some Pembrokeshire and especially Fishguard and Goodwick housewives that they occasionally do their shopping in another country, that is, they make a profitable shopping expedition during a twenty-four-hours' visit to Ireland.

Lower Fishguard retains its ancient character as a haven for small boats, and is the centre for the local sailing club. It is highly picturesque when first seen by the visitor descending the steep hill from Fishguard itself towards the bridge over the river Gwaun (pronounced "Gwyne"), resembling some Cornish or Breton small port.

The Welsh name of Fishguard is Abergwaun. The recent revival of Welsh place-names, supported by a majority of the Pembrokeshire County Council after heated debates in the council chamber, is everywhere evident in the north, where the signposts at the approach to village or town often give both the Welsh and English names.

In Lower Fishguard, tucked away at the end of the road leading up the Gwaun valley, is the mansion built by Fenton, author of *A Historical Tour Through Pembrokeshire* (1811). From this book many later writers have drawn pabulum for an account of Pembrokeshire; he is a favourite with local men and women, but as some of his statements have been proved inaccurate, the more honest historians have been wary of accepting him without reservation.

Fenton was born at St David's, where the Cathedral register records he was baptised "Feb 20, 1747, Richard, the son of Richard and Martha Fenton, being then a month old". He became a law student, was a moderate poet, and knew Oliver Goldsmith, Edmund Burke, Joshua Reynolds, and Samuel Johnson while at "the academic fountain of Oxford". He also knew David Garrick, who gave him the freedom of his theatre. Reynolds painted the portraits of Fenton and his beautiful wife, Eloise la Baronne Pillet de Mondon, upon ivory miniatures.

Fenton's liaison with this Frenchwoman came about as the result of a caprice of Goldsmith. As the two young men were strolling one summer afternoon along the lanes of Marylebone, then a fashionable country suburb, they noticed a party of ladies at tea in the garden of a fine villa. Fenton was so struck by the rare beauty of one of the young women that he stopped to get another view of her—and fell in love completely. Goldsmith, summing up the situation on Fenton declaring that this was the ideal woman he would want to, nay must, marry, declared he was an old friend of the family and would introduce him forthwith. Dragging Fenton into the garden he went up to a military-looking gentleman presiding over the ladies and introduced "Mr. Fenton, the celebrated Welsh poet!" They were invited to tea, discussed the world in perfect French, and left after Fenton had chatted to his future wife. Afterwards, when challenged by Fenton, Goldsmith admitted he had never met the family before, did not even know their names, but had gate-crashed simply to enable Fenton to meet a pretty girl. The infatuated Fenton followed up the introduction gained and discovered his future wife to be daughter of Col. Pillet de Mondon, a Swiss who was secretary to the Duke of Marlborough.

The house he built in the green valley of the Gwaun for Eloise was known as Glynamel. But Fenton's connections with Fishguard had begun earlier: he was called there to help his uncle the merchant-shipowner Samuel Fenton, who, childless, wished Richard to carry on the prosperous shipping and fishery he had built up in the port of Lower Fishguard (which he had himself constructed). At that time pilchards visited the Welsh coast in great numbers and Samuel Fenton set about curing and exporting the catches of local fishermen. A hundred years later pilchards (a pilchard is an adult sardine) no longer visited Welsh waters in great shoals and the fishery has since quite died out.

When the foundation stone of Glynamel was ready to be laid, Richard called a *cymanfa* or general meeting of neighbours, to wish him well and consecrate the site. The priest having pronounced the blessing and Fenton having addressed the crowd, suddenly a Welsh woman came forward and in hysterical terms denounced Fenton for having taken from her the meadow, promised her by his uncle as a reward for nursing services, on which the new house was being built. She cursed him and his children and his new home and prophesied that his plans for the future would fail and all misfortune be his from the day he entered his new home.

This incident had a profound effect on the assembly and upon Fenton himself, although he declared he had not heard before of his uncle's promise. As if afraid of the curse he granted the woman a life lease, as from Anne Eynon herself, by which he paid her £30 per annum for the field in which the house and grounds were established, and also gave her and her daughter a cottage and garden rent free for life. In spite of this, Anne Eynon's prophecy was fulfilled. His eldest son John quarrelled with him and Fenton left the estate to the next son, who sold it back to John, who in turn dissipated it completely.

Earlier, during the American War of Independence, the famous pirate Paul Jones entered Fishguard roads in his privateer, and seized one of Sam Fenton's merchant ships. He then sent an armed party ashore to demand 500 guineas ransom in spot cash, or the ship would be sunk; and from the inhabitants of the Upper Town a similar ransom was demanded, in default of which the place would be bombarded. The ransoms were paid but not before a warning shot or two had damaged the town and by ill-luck struck and lamed for life Richard Fenton's sister Mary.

Glynamel is still occupied, with much of its old gardens well maintained, but not by a Fenton. The estate sits astride the narrow lovely lower reaches of the wooded ravine of the Gwaun Valley. There is no way for a car to penetrate the valley for several miles upstream. No doubt in time this part will be opened to traffic under the developing National Park so that entry can be made from Fishguard's Lower Town; meanwhile the beautiful hanging woods and slopes are the undisturbed home of the buzzard, badger, fox and even polecat, and the valley is worth traversing from end to end without artificial aids.

The Gwaun is famous for trout and sea-trout (locally called sewin), as are all three Pembrokeshire small rivers—Taf, Cleddau, and Nevern. One of the most satisfying walks is to take the lane on the west side of the Gwaun bridge at Fishguard and stroll upstream through the pass opposite Glynamel, following the Gwaun to Picton Mill Bridge, under the residence of ancient Pontfaen, noble-looking on its high eminence. Thence take the road northwards over Dinas Mountain (Mynydd Dinas), a wild gorse and heather and stone waste with the most glorious views of the Cardigan Bay coast, Fishguard harbour and the mountains of north Wales and Bardsey Island, and southwards to the west Pembrokeshire islands. On a clear day the Wicklow Mountains of Ireland are visible to the north-west.

If the walk can be extended one ought to follow the stone-strewn ridge eastwards (by good paths and prehistoric tracks at intervals) from Dinas Mountain to the crown of Carningli (Rock of Angels), where hill foxes lurk among the stone walls and the hut-circles of an ancient British encampment overlooking Newport. Or else one might descend—on a summer day—to bathe in one or other of the sandy bays which pincer the isthmus under (what is really the peninsula of) Dinas Island.

There is an inn at Pwllgwaelod, at the west side of the isthmus: the *Sailor's Safety* has a clientele from all over Pembrokeshire, because of its good service and pleasant position beside this isolated beach, and partly perhaps because of tales of the smuggling that was formerly indulged there—tales which add to its romantic air. On the east side is Cwm-yr-eglwys (the church in the coomb), whose sheltered sandy beach is a favourite with children. Here the sea has eaten away the church and churchyard: it is said that the eastern part of the church with the altar and chancel disappeared into the sea during a great storm which raged one Sunday during the evening service—a novel by Mr Hay graphically describes this alarming and improbable occasion.

Dinas Island, rising to 463 feet from the sea, is a large farm of over 400 acres, one of the few facing south on this north coast, and for that reason it catches the sun, dries quickly and produces early crops. For eight years I farmed it myself, and my only regret is that I was not content to stay in so magical a spot for the rest of my life: for it has all that a farmer and naturalist could desire, including sea-birds and seals which were not mentioned in the inventory when I took over. Many a summer's day, when the work in the fields was over, my family sailed with me in our 24-foot Irish curragh, visiting the sea-birds on the Needle Rock, or entering the long cave near Pwll-glas where in deep darkness the seals bear their calves on beaches far under the island's massive walls. Black cattle and speckle-faced Kerry Hill sheep, corn and early potatoes were raised. In spite of much rock outcropping on the slopes the Island Farm has always been highly productive. It was in Elizabethan days kept as a grange, or game outfarm, to the house of Pentre Ifan "for the better maintenance of hospitality", according to George Owen.

Pentre Evan itself, once a noble mansion, near Newport, has faded away to be replaced by an insignificant farmhouse. The name is today associated with the nearby cromlech or burial chamber, one of the finest surviving in Britain, lying on the lower slopes of Prescelly, and now in the care of the Ministry of Works. Fenton regarded it as "the largest Druidical relic in Wales". George Owen in 1603 made a plan of the "gromlech" which is copied in Laws' book.

The Druidical connection with cromlechs and stone circles has for the present been discredited, in spite of which the elaborate gorsedd (stone circle) ceremonies of the modern eisteddfoddau of the Welsh people of today, which were founded on this myth, still continue, complete with druids and arch-druids, and bardic honours and crowns. As for Pentre-Ifan, it is a communal burial chamber, built perhaps in 2000 B.C. by the Iberian-Mediterranean colonists who brought their megalithic culture to the west coast at that time. W. F. Grimes, who excavated the site, found fragments of pottery, in a charcoal deposit, which were from a round-bottomed bowl of normal neolithic type A. Usually these cromlechs were buried under an earth mound; and some still are—as the magnificent Hougue Bie in Jersey which was so well concealed under a majestic mound (upon which stood an old chapel) that it was not discovered and opened until 1924.

Yet some smaller cromlechs in Pembrokeshire and along the western seaboard are upon such rocky, soil-less sites that they would appear never to have been covered; one might surmise that these inferior windswept chambers were the burial vaults and ritual sites of lesser priests or chieftains of invading megalithic tribes. The earth that covered such a cromlech, if ever it did completely, was perhaps not much more than a sprinkling, or perhaps a pile of stones laboriously carried by the mourners, slaves, and others obliged by fear and faith to secure the dead from both human and animal carrion hunters.

Back now to Newport, a little town of 1,250 inhabitants, most of them peacefully employed in catering for the farming and holiday interests. A Welsh-speaking community in winter, Newport nearly doubles its population with the summer invasion of English visitors who find the combination of fine sands, and a hinterland of little whitewashed farmhouses, mountain and moor to their discerning taste. On the slope overlooking the town is Newport Castle, partly a ruin but with the north end, which gazes seaward, occupied and in good order, and at the time I write this, a guest house.

Newport Castle was built by the adventuring Norman knight Martin de Turribus, who came by sea to Pembrokeshire from Devon and Somerset where he had gained lands in the Norman conquest of England. He landed at Fishguard, subdued or drove to the mountains the poorly armed Welsh, and set up as a Lord Marcher over the whole of north-east Pembrokeshire.

His grandson William Martin married Angharad, daughter of the Lord Rhys ap Gruffudd ap Rhys ap Tewdwr (to give her line of descent from the ruling princes of south Wales. The word "ap" means "son of").

Thus was founded the Marcher Lordship of Kemes or Cemaes, a Norman sub-kingdom almost of its own in the heart of the Welshery, and at first ruled despotically under military law. No Welshman was allowed a vote or could become a burgess. The right of appointing officials was that of the Marcher Lord, and to this day his descendant has the right to appoint the Mayor of Newport.

St Margaret's Isle, from the west end of Caldey Island. St Margaret's is a sea-bird sanctuary administered by the West Wales Field Society

The monastery on Caldey Island, built by Benedictines, but now occupied by Cistercian monks

George Owen gives a long description of the Welsh game of ball or *knappan*, peculiar to the neighbourhood of Newport. It was played by an unlimited company both on foot and on horseback. Parish against parish contended for possession of a wooden ball which Owen describes as of sufficient size only to be held in one fist. It must be of heavy wood such as box, yew, crab-apple or holly, and it had to be boiled in tallow to make it slippery. The object of the game was to carry the knappan as far as possible into the heart of the home parish, away from the parish of the opponent, either by throwing it from one to another or by carrying it oneself, as in rugby football. Knappan was in fact a kind of rugby football without boundaries. Rules were made, slightly barbaric perhaps. The footmen were permitted to use their fists, and the horsemen cudgels of hazel, upon any opponent who would not yield the knappan when challenged, that is, if they could catch him. Owen complains that nowadays (he was writing about the year 1600) the rules were little observed, the horsemen carried "monstrouse cudgells" of oak, and the footmen worked off "privatt grudges" so that

"for everye small occasion they fall by the eares, wch beinge once kindled betweene two, all persons on both sides become parties, soe that sometymes you shall see fyve or vi hundred naked men, beatinge in a clusture together, as fast as the fiste can goe, and there parte most be taken everyeman with his companie, soe that you shall see two brothers the on beateinge the other, the man the maister, and frinde against frinde, they nowe alsoe will not stick to take upp stones and there with in theire fistes beate theire fellowes, the horsemen will intrude and ryde into the footemens troupes, the horseman choseth the greatest cudgell he can gett, and the same of oke, ashe, blackthorne or crab-tree, and soe huge as it were able to strike downe an oxe or horse . . .".

Yet, after these bastinadoes and wholesale settlements of private grudges in the heat of knappan

"you shall see gamesters retorne home from this playe with broken heads, black faces, brused bodies, and lame legges,

7   97

A typical colour-washed farm steading of Dewisland, with round (miscalled Flemish) chimney

Interlaced cross stone, Nevern church

yett laugheinge & merylie jestinge at theire harmes, tellinge theire adversaries how he brake his heade to an other that he strake him on the face, and howe he repaied the same to him againe, all this in good mirthe, without grudge or hatred, and if anye be in arrerages to the other they store it upp till the next plaie, and in the meane tyme will contynue loveinge frindes, whereas if the least of these blowes be offred out of this plaie, it presentlye breedeth vnquenchable quarrells, by this you see the horsemens game is right horse playe, and theire lawe plaine Stafford lawe [the law of the stick—R.M.L.]".

George Owen was born at Henllys, near Nevern, in 1552, and died there in 1612. There he wrote his three books of "the description of Penbrockshire" in the copper-plate style of the best writers of his day, neat, with broad strokes and flourishes of his quill-pen, yet withal most legible.

He was Lord of Kemes through the pertinacity of his father William Owen, who after nineteen years of litigation, won back the barony for his family following the treason, ending in execution in 1497, of Lord Audley, who had inherited it by the female line through a sister of a Martin, direct descendant of Martin de Tours. William Owen's claim to the barony of Cemaes and castle of Newport was as a descendant of Ales, only daughter of Nicholas Martin, Lord of Kemes. But George Owen preferred to dwell at Henllys, home of his Welsh forbears who were descended in direct male line from Rhys ap Tewdwr, the last king of south Wales.

Henllys today is a modernised farm with little of the great house of Owen in evidence in the remains of walls and foundations, though it still commands a noble prospect over the steep Nevern valley, with its singing salmon and sewin stream where otters whistle by night. Here George Owen lived in patriarchal style, having eight or ten children by his first, and twelve by his second, wife. At the entrance to the valley up which winds the steep road to Henllys lies Velindre, a pretty hamlet which still contains the little court house (college) where Owen, as Lord of Kemes, may have held baronial court to try local cases of slander and small debts: it is I believe used today for the "court leet", where burgesses of Newport hear cases to do with infringement of the rights of the commoners who graze the open mountain and moor in Cemaes.

Opposite the gate to Henllys is that of Cwmgloyne, described by Fenton as one of the few ancient houses, which formerly besprinkled the Cemaes district and lordship in great number, not yet metamorphosed into a farmhouse—in 1800. It was a noble building even in 1940 when I first saw it as the farmhouse of a derelict farm which I subsequently rented for a song on condition that I would restore the farm. All the land here is up hill or down dale, wild and near to the bone of the slate rock; not fertile, yet kind to the eye of a naturalist. On each stone pillar of the entrance gate to Cwmgloyne used to be an ancient gargoylish stone face, one of which was lately smashed by a passing lorry. The old house had a great kitchen and cellars under a panelled hall. During my occupation of this house I pulled away a modern stove which had blocked the entrance to a vast hearth in the kitchen. This revealed an old wall baking-oven in which I found books nearly one hundred and fifty years old: Marshall's *Agriculture* and a farm account book of 1750 with many entries curious to a modern farmer. In the huge chimney could be discerned, above lintel height, a walled-in doorway with, if I remember aright, a pointed arch. We called this the priests' chamber: according to local hearsay belief it was used as such during the Reformation, as hideouts in several local manors and churches were said to be.

The clear spring issuing from the rock at Cwmgloyne flows through a steep wooded ravine containing a beautiful drive from lodge gates in the hamlet of Velindre: but the woods have lately been felled and the lodge become roofless, and in the general levelling of human society, Cwmgloyne, like many another late medieval manor, is now an ordinary farm.

Some of these old manor-sites, if not occupied by milk-producing farmers, have become guest-houses. Such is Llwyngwair, near Newport, which has been the seat of the Bowen (ap Owen) family for many centuries; it is most happily situated by the banks of the clear Nevern river in a bower of woods which in spring are strewn with anemones, primroses and daffodils.

Nevern itself is one of the prettiest and oldest of hamlets, hidden in a fold of the river valley. On the heights above is the ruin of a great Welsh chieftain's castle of unknown age; it was destroyed by Martin de Turribus in the Norman invasion. Earlier, in the fifth century A.D., the evangelical children of an invading Irish gael chieftain had settled hereabouts in north Pembrokeshire and brought Christianity to Cemaes. Here Brynach, the Irish husband of Cymorth, daughter of this chieftain, founded seven churches: Llanfyrnach, Llanboidy, Kilymaen-llwyd, Henry's Moat, Pontfaen, Dinas and Nevern.

The present fine church has a squat late-Perpendicular tower and a chancel curiously out of line with the nave. In the church-yard very old yews weep "blood" from their cut gnarled arms; there is a tradition that until the native Welsh chieftainship is restored to ruined Nevern castle, the soil must silently protest against the presence of alien feet. The visitor will find the red sap of the yews dripping upon conveniently placed slate slabs.

St Brynach's Cross stands 13 feet high in the churchyard, an early Christian Ogham monument beautifully carved with end-less "love-knot" patterns. There is also a Roman legionary camp-site stone, removed from a field on Cwmgloyne Farm. Within the building of the church is a separate sanctuary with accom-modation (refectory and dormitory) for a small religious community, which is said to have been used last during the Reformation.

Rivalling the St David's Head coastline, the high cliffs of the Newport Head to Cemaes Head shore are wild and beautiful, noted for wild flowers and sea-birds, without a building of any kind until the little fishermen's inlet of Ceibwr is reached. Follow the stream here to the village of Moylgrove, in order to reach the dolmen Llech-y-Dribedd.

Returning north along the coast, over a path above majestic cliffs, above shingle beaches, caves, arches, syncline and anti-cline in the exposed shale, to reach Cemaes Head with its views south to Dinas and north to Cardigan Island, and around Cardigan Bay to Snowdon and Bardsey Island.

Cardigan Island, 40 acres of grass and low cliff, at present a sanctuary for a flock of St Kildan sheep, pillars the Cardiganshire side of the entrance to the Teify river. On the Pembrokeshire side lie Poppit Sands, a favourite local bathing beach. The old fishing village of St Dogmaels commands the scene a few miles upriver, looking down from the hill upon calm Teify Pool, where the salmon net-men moor their boats. This is a charming spot, and close by are the ruins of the Barnadine abbey founded by Robert de Turribus in 1115.

I had nearly forgotten to mention that two breeds of dog originated in North Pembrokeshire: the Corgi and the Sealyham. The latter was evolved at Sealyham, a country house south of Fishguard which is now a convalescent home, by a master of foxhounds, Captain Jack Edwardes, about 1860. It was a cross between the Corgi and rough-haired terriers, including the Dandie Dinmont.

The Pembrokeshire Corgi is much older. It is believed to date from the introduction of the Swedish Vallhund, carried to South Wales by Viking raiders and settlers. It is mentioned in Welsh literature as far back as Hywel Dda.

CHAPTER VIII

MILFORD HAVEN

"MILFORD HAVEN is one of the finest as well as the most scenically attractive harbours in the world." How often is not this boast heard or written in local as well as national circles. Lord Nelson considered it and Trincomalee in Ceylon the finest harbours he had ever seen. Yet, except during war, it was neglected by the world's shipping. It was not situated close enough to any industrial centre to attract ships. It was known by choice or by chance to the discerning holidaying visitor, to some personnel from naval and air establishments, to those employed in its trawling fishery at Milford itself, and to the "English" natives along its red sandstone shores.

Both the town and the whole magnificent sunken estuary from St Ann's Head as far as salt flows to Haverfordwest are known as Milford Haven, though properly Milford or Milford Dock would be a more sensible name for the town. But "Haven" is tagged on to distinguish the town from so many other Milfords in the British Isles.

With a 25-foot rise inside the Haven, the sea at high water spring tides penetrates some twenty-five miles into the heart of the county. This lovely interior coastline is nearly one hundred miles long, with fine bays or high water lakes and safe anchorages at Dale, Angle, Sandy Haven, Pennar, Cosheston, Carew, Creselly, Llangwm, and the Western and Eastern Cleddaus. Ships of up to 6 feet draught can navigate at high springs to the quay at Haverfordwest and to Blackpool Mill, where the mountain streams bounce over seaweed-draped boulders at the ebb of the tide.

The Vikings came up to Haverfordwest in their double-prowed ships, the Normans came to Pembroke, the Flemings traded in and out of the Haven, George Owen surveyed it, and there are many records of cargoes and ships that had to do with Milford from the sixteenth century to the present day. There is

102

an interesting record of February 2nd, 1567, when the sailing vessel *Le Turtaile de Milford* (Master, Arnold William) left "the town of Milford" with a cargo owned by merchants Thomas Verdon and Patrick Ferris, for Bristol and consisting of "800 sheep skins, 400 lamb pelts, 60 st. floks, 30 st. wool, 10 dikers hides, 40 barrels herrings, 8 fkns. salmon". A good mixture of the local farming and fishing products, but at that date the present town of Milford did not exist; Neyland was known as Milford Haven until 1859, and as New Milford until 1906.

This haven had been alive with shipping for hundreds of years right down to the appearance of the first small steam craft one hundred years ago which had not yet displaced the fleets of barques and barges, schooners, ketches and wooden sailing ships which carried anthracite from the mines at Hook, stones from the limestone quarries along the eastern shore, and farmers' corn from a dozen inland quays. (It was estimated that 20 thousand tons of anthracite were transhipped annually 1681–90.) There were busy rowboat ferries at Landshipping, Langwm, Lawrenny, Pembroke–Burton, and Neyland–Hobbs Point. The last is the only regular surviving ferry, now a motor-boat service run by the County Council.

Road transport and the closing of the Hook colliery completely killed the uphaven trade. When I first came to live on Skokholm Island in 1927 there were still many small schooners and ketches, some motorised, carrying cargoes of up to 50 tons of anthracite. With a fresh easterly wind after a westerly gale these ships, lately weatherbound, would sail out at the turn of the tide in a fine fleet, racing up through the sounds in the direction of Ireland. In Pembrokeshire we knew this fleet half-admiringly, half-derisively, as the Irish Navy.

In ten years the fleet had vanished. Year by year it had grown more ragged as patched sails gave way to bare poles with the white puff of engine exhaust behind. The uphaven waters today are bare of commercial craft, but small pleasure boats—motor-cruisers, sailing dinghies, and rowing and outboard open boats—increase each year, while here and there the last of the sailing schooners and ketches lie rotting in some side creek or "pill".

The waters north of Pembroke Dock are the playground of those who love to mess about in and fish from small boats, in reasonable shelter and free from the Atlantic swell. The strong tide is a good servant to those who plan to use it on the inland voyages, but it can be a bad master to those who don't, stranding them on mud or rock or fighting them with a five-knot stream.

At Llangwm, the inhabitants formerly lived exclusively by fishing. Cockles, oysters and mud clams or mussels were collected at low tide from the thick ugly tarred Llangwm boats grounded on the shellfish beds. The Llangwm boat is the modern equivalent of the primitive early British osier and hide coracle or currach. The shellfishery has petered out, but net-fishing for salmon, bass, mullet and herring in season still continues. The salmon are taken in sweep, lave or tip nets, each man standing in his little boat and "feeling" for a fish along the bottom with a net fixed to two long poles, on a rising tide.

The Llangwm women were famous for their toughness. Right into the present century they would stone strangers from their village—probably this can be traced back to their Welsh origin which made them fearful of visits from the Norse, Norman and Saxon invaders occupying the country around them. Llangwm women used to walk regularly, with heavy baskets of fish, to Tenby, Pembroke and other towns, being ferried across the haven by their husbands or themselves, for even the women were capable in a boat, and were said to dominate their men.

Modern Llangwm is a pleasant village of white houses; it won the 1955 competition for the most attractive and well kept village in Pembrokeshire. Its environment is enchanting. North of the village the Haven (Cleddau) splits, each tributary winding east or west amid green fields and woods. The eastern Cleddau passes beneath the castles and demesnes of Picton and Slebech towards Black Pool. South of Llangwm is the open Beggar's Reach, then the wooded narrows of Castle Reach with ancient Benton Castle in the western wood, and Lawrenny quay (Lawrenny castle now competely dismantled) on the east side, a wharf catering for the convenience of visitors and yachts, and opening upon the broad Cresswell or Carew River.

For years a dispute raged (and still rages at intervals) in the Pembrokeshire Press on the alternatives of building dam or bridge to replace the much-derided Neyland–Hobbs Point ferry. A public enquiry ended somewhat abortively, although the Admiralty declared itself neutral, provided naval vessels could pass through the barrage or under the bridge. There are those who believe that a dam carrying the main road, with locks for ships to pass through, would "make" Pembrokeshire, by creating a permanent inland lake ideal for boating and fishing—a rival to the Norfolk Broads. But there are others, many of them residing beside the waters of the haven, who will not give up their tidal water at any price. The costs of building a dam or a bridge are about equal, although the annual upkeep of a steel bridge, high enough to clear a sea-going vessel's masts, would probably be excessive.

As to Milford itself, it is the youngest of towns and boroughs in the county, a modern child indeed compared to its nearest rival, the borough of Pembroke of comparable population. While ancient British, Norse and Norman and other, often piratical, traffic flowed in and out of the Haven over the wild tide-races of St Ann's Head the site of Milford Town remained a near-uninhabited peaceful farmland of creek and field where, at most, ships' boats might occasionally put in for fresh water.

The advent of the Spanish Armada (1588) caused uneasiness in government circles leading to an examination of the Haven's possibilities for defence, which was conducted efficiently by George Owen, Deputy Lieutenant of Pembrokeshire, whose description is on record. He recommended that forts should be built on Thorn Island, Dale Point, and the Stack Rock in the centre of the haven. These forts were not built until nearly 300 years had elapsed! Meanwhile the only battle was in 1644, when Parliamentary ships under Captain Swanley attacked the Royalists near the old chapel of St Thomas at the mouth of Castle Pill, Milford, and took 7 captains, 300 men, 18 great ordnance and 6 field carriages in a total surrender.

West of Castle Pill lies Priory Pill, so called because of the eleventh-century priory of Benedictine monks, the remains of

whose house still stand. (It was in this pill or creek that my grandfather had his sawmill business.) The modern town of Milford
was begun on the breast of the hill which separates the two pills.
At the dissolution of the monasteries in the sixteenth century the
lands about Hubberston and Pill manors had come into the possession of the Barlow family. The wealthy heiress Catherine Barlow
married Sir William Hamilton, who outlived her and enjoyed her
fortune. Sir William was sixty-one in 1791 when he married
the twenty-six-year-old beauty, Amy Lyon (Emma Hart). The
artist Romney was a friend of Sir William, and painted the famous studies of the young wife about this time.

The enterprising Sir William secured an Act of Parliament in
1790 to enable him to "make and provide Quays, Docks, Piers
and other erections" at Hubberston and Pill, for which purpose
he employed his energetic nephew, Charles Frances Greville (a
son of the Earl of Warwick) to act as superintendent. Greville
canvassed all persons he could attract to help him in building the
new port, including the Quaker whalers who had come to Britain
during the War of American Independence. He secured at least
two of these families, the Folgers and the Starbucks, who owned
five whaling barquentines: it was intended to base these on the
new "docks" at Milford. Greville also secured orders for the
building of two naval men-of-war: the *Milford* of seventy-eight,
and the *Lavinia* of forty-eight, guns.

Sir William inspected progress in the summer of 1801, and was
alarmed to find it was necessary to raise about £10,000 to complete the docks, piers, etc. (He was, by now, no longer a happy
husband. His second wife had set herself to secure the attentions
of his friend Lord Nelson.) In a letter to Greville after the visit,
however, Sir William reassures his nephew of his trust in all his
operations of building the new sea-port. In July 1802 he and his
wife and Nelson arrived in time for the anniversary celebrations
of the Battle of the Nile, which included a grand fair and agricultural show and a regatta. Nelson delivered an enthusiastic
speech, praising Greville for all: the whaling and shipbuilding
industry, the Custom House, and the Irish mail packet daily
service.

Parties at Picton Castle, Stackpole Court, Tenby, etc., followed. Lady Hamilton was subjected to severe criticism for her improper behaviour, but seemed to regard her double role as a great triumph. Sir William, who was in poor health, died nine months later, and was by his own wish buried beside his first wife, Catherine, at Slebech.

The determined Greville, now tenant of the Pembrokeshire estates of Sir William, went ahead with the building of Milford. He began the church (dedicated to St Katherine) in 1803, but it was not consecrated until four years later. He determined upon a technical college with leanings towards engineering and navigation and survey; of this project only an astronomical observatory appears to have been finally completed. Nor did he live to complete a dock but only a quay which was left dry at the ebb. He died in 1809, and thereafter the new town of Milford sadly lacked its pioneer who believed so whole-heartedly in it.

Sir Frederick Rees has written *The Story of Milford*, for clarifying which every writer on the subject, must be, like myself, grateful. He describes how Greville's brother Robert Fulke, an equerry and a man about town and hunting field, on succeeding to the Pembrokeshire interests, was told by his wife, the widowed Countess of Mansfield, that "Milford had better remain as cornfields" rather than their fortune be spent on further development; and there followed an attempt by this couple, disastrous for the new town, to exploit the position so laboriously gained by Charles Greville. The Navy Board, which rented a yard at Milford, offered to purchase the site for £4,455, a price already agreed by Charles Greville. Robert refusing, the naval establishment was transferred to Pembroke Dock (then known as Paterchurch).

This loss, and the decline in the whale fishery, led to a state of stagnation in the new town, further aggravated by the transference in 1836 of the Irish mail packet station to Hobbs Point (Paterchurch). There was nothing much left except the shipbuilding and victualling. As to the shipbuilding, my grandfather's firm about this time began to supply timber for this and other local requirements. The business—Williams (my great uncle) & Mathias—was established in Priory Pill, up which timber ships could unload their cargoes, and local timber, brought by horse-drawn or steam wagon, arrived by road. Many a stout elm keel and oak knees and stems came from woods in the sheltered western Welsh valleys.

The Docks, which closed in the waters of Priory Pill, were not finally completed until 1888, and at great expense, but then great rewards were expected to follow: it had always been planned that Milford would be the west-coast harbour for future transatlantic traffic (in place of Liverpool) now that the Great Western Railway served the town. Prophetically the first ship to enter the dock, on September 27th, 1888, was the steam trawler *Sibyl*. And to this day Milford Docks has had to rely on steam trawlers and other small fishing craft for its prosperity.

Milford trawlers exploit chiefly the hake-fishery of the west coast, especially the south-west coast of Ireland. Herrings are landed, in season, by the itinerant East Coast steam and motor drifters.

★　　★　　★　　★　　★

For the yachtsman and those who like to explore in small boats, Milford Haven cannot be equalled in England and Wales. There are perhaps havens and harbours as good in Scotland and Ireland, but not with a more equable and sunny climate.

On entering by St Ann's Head, the best time is just on the flood after low water, and the worst at full tide when the stream rushes forth and if the wind is westerly creates heavy overfalls.

On the north shore Watwick, Mill and Castlebeach bays are all good in a north wind for a short spell at anchor—to clear up after a long voyage or for a picnic and a bathe. In a southerly wind Dale Roads is a safe anchorage, quite close under the trees of Point Wood. The converted Fort on Dale Point is now a centre for open air studies and administered by the Field Studies Council, which conducts there field courses for naturalists and students of biology. Dale itself is a lobster-fishing village lying in the isthmus; its old-world charm has lately been spoilt by the erection of modern houses for naval air arm personnel. It has an inn, one or two shops, a castle and a late Norman-type tower to its little church. It takes its name from the Norman overlord, De Vale. At high water small boats can reach the quay wall outside the Griffin Inn.

Proceeding north along the coast Sandy Haven is a beautiful unspoilt inlet, accessible at high tide by a channel up to a private quay (the Sloop Inn), by wood and pasture, where a boat can lie comfortably on gravel over the low tide. Thence there are walks to the village of St Ishmaels (two miles) with shops, on the west side, and to the hamlet of Herbrandston on the east.

The triangle of sea between Dale, Sandy Haven and Angle is the best sea-fishing area inside the haven. Mackerel abound from July to October, with plenty of mullet, bass and pollack coming to lines or nets.

Angle on the south side is safer than Dale, though it dries out and the inner harbour and ancient battered quay are accessible only for a few hours at high water. Like Dale it lies in a hollow between sea and sea, but is more sheltered and less populated: one of the best bases in the Haven, if you can wait on the tide, for a leisurely yachting holiday, for it is handy to the open sea and to the uphaven water alike. At low tide cockles can be collected on foot over the sands of the great bay of Angle.

Sailing eastwards from Angle, past Popton Point (a former Victorian fort) one passes the ocean terminal piers of the B.P. and Regent Oil Companies. Next, Pennar Gut leads towards the village of Hundleton, and round the corner, amid farm fields and trees, to Pembroke Castle, Mill and Quay, where the boat can lie on soft mud at high water.

Pennar Gut, like Angle, Dale, Cosheston, Lawrenny, Garron Pill, Norchard and all the other pills and creeks up to Haverfordwest and to Slebech, abounds with wild fowl in winter, especially wigeon, teal, mallard, sheld-duck and numerous wading birds. The Pembrokeshire men have always had a taste for duck-shooting and many of the ducks caught, ring-marked and released by us at Orielton Decoy have been shot soon after in or near Milford Haven. In the summer the same ducks travel far to eastern breeding grounds in Europe and Russia.

The herring shoals in winter and early spring travel up to

Llangwm, where the salmon fishermen catch them in nets. Often Atlantic seals, porpoises and dolphins follow the shoals as far as Castle and Beggars' Reaches. Common dolphins and bottle-nosed dolphins have been identified by their shape and colour when they leap clear of the sea in sportive exuberance—and a fine sight it is to see these great creatures bounding in parabolic leaps in the sheltered waters of the Haven.

Another fine sight within the last few years is that of the procession of the world's largest ships, chiefly oil tankers up to and above 100,000 tons, entering and leaving the haven. These are bringing crude oil to the wharves of the new refineries and their pipe-lines. Leading oil companies such as British Petroleum, Esso and Regent are now established on each side of the tide-scoured channel of this magnificent water-way, said to be the deepest in the British Isles. Nelson's remarks—quoted above—assume their fullest significance for the first time. Thanks to careful siting and planning restrictions much of this new industry, saving the tall smoke and flare stacks, does not intrude upon the eye of the tourist—so far. May it ever be so.

CHAPTER IX

CASTLES AND PALACES

THE oldest sites of historic, as distinct from prehistoric, buildings in Pembrokeshire must be those associated with the Celtic saints: the sites of their cells and chapels. Of these the best known is the sixth-century monastic settlement of St David's, in the valley of the Alun stream, Vallis Rosina or in Welsh, Glyn Rhosin, where the present cathedral stands. Nothing remains to view of this important monastic house and early bishopric: it was utterly destroyed in the eleventh century by Viking raiders and for seven years lay waste; even the tomb of St David was so covered with brambles that a visiting pilgrim took seven days to hack open a route to it.

In 1081 William the Conqueror made his pilgrimage to St David's, incidentally receiving the homage of the Welsh Prince Rhys, the ruler of Dyfed (south-west Wales), on whose death twelve years later the Normans took a firmer grip of the bishopric. In 1115 Bernard, the Queen's Chancellor, was made bishop of St David's. About this time the first substantial cathedral must have been completed.

The fact that two pilgrimages to St David's were held to equal one to Rome seems to have encouraged kings, noblemen and magnates to visit the cathedral, although in the case of royalty it was also a showing of the English colours among the ever restless and rebellious Welsh.

Henry II in 1172, and Edward I and his Queen in 1284, are examples of these visits, which doubtless stimulated bishops to improve the accommodation of their palace. The master masons were kept busy on both cathedral and palace for another century or more. Bishop Henry de Gower, a nobleman from Glamorganshire, is believed to have been responsible (1327-47) for the richly decorated style, with arcaded parapets and rose windows, to be seen in the present cathedral and bishop's palace—as well as in the smaller palace—a country seat of the bishop—at Lamphey, south Pembrokeshire. Bishop Gower lies in a canopied tomb by the fine screen he himself erected and which separates nave and choir.

Soon after the Reformation the palaces were allowed to decay, and under Bishop Barlow (1536-48) the lead from the roof of the main hall at St David's was stripped, and the episcopal base was transferred to Abergwili, near the more populous town of Carmarthen.

The Norman bishops of St David's also possessed the barony and fortified moated castle of Llawhaden, which lies nobly on an eminence above the Eastern Cleddau, commanding the central eastern approaches of the county. Llawhaden—which is locally pronounced "low-adden"—was built in the heyday of Norman supremacy in the late thirteenth–early fourteenth century. The two great drum-towers of the gatehouse and the stair tower to the chapel are the main survivals of this fortress, now in the care of the Ministry of Works. In 1402 Henry IV issued authority to the bishop to garrison Llawhaden against the raiding parties of the Welsh prince Owain Glyndwr.

There is a story that Bishop John Morgan (about 1503) seized a certain lady Tanglost and imprisoned her at Llawhaden, because of her ill fame. Thomas Wyriott of Orielton came to her rescue with mounted troops and successfully stormed the castle. But the woman, persisting in her wicked ways, was once again imprisoned and Wyriott now asked the bishop to pardon them both. On her release Tanglost went to Bristol and engaged a witch to put a spell on the bishop. Waxen effigies of the prelate were made and stuck full of pins. Hearing of this, the bishop was frightened and appealed to the "Mayor and Corporation" of Bristol to convict Tanglost. All ended well: Tanglost repented and reformed forthwith. Soon after this, Bishop Barlow despoiled Llawhaden by stripping the lead off the roof, as he had done to St David's palace, in his efforts to move the see to Carmarthen.

The present cathedral of St David's requires a full day to explore, for as we have seen it has a long history of destruction, and of repair, beginning with the day of its foundation by the

Carew Cheriton church, like many late Norman churches in south Pembrokeshire, has a tall tower which served the purpose of a military watch-post

CARREG GOFFA
GLANLLYN FFARMDID
CHWEFROR 22 1797

MEMORIAL STONE
— OF THE —
LANDING OF THE FRENCH
FEBRUARY 22 1797

1897

saint whose tomb it enshrines. The outside is plain, almost dull, due to the uninspiring purplish rock from the cliff-quarries of Caerbwdy. Inside, the great arches of the late Norman period are striking; noble columns alternately octagonal and round, with detached shafts. The nave is the work of Peter de Leia (1180). The original tower, which was low enough to be hidden in the valley out of sight of passing ships, collapsed in 1220, the foundations of the cathedral having been laid in a swamp. In 1248 an earthquake tumbled down the east end of the cathedral.

The roof, with its exquisite tracery, is of Irish oak, about 450 years old. The Lady Chapel was built about 1300. Underneath the great tower is the choir with twenty-eight stalls (c. 1470), including one reserved for the Sovereign and occupied by Queen Elizabeth II on her visit in 1955. Underneath the stalls are ludicrous miserichord carvings. The floor to the high altar is of tiles bearing escutcheons and mottoes, and the richly painted ceiling bears the coats of arms of benefactors. On the left is the remains of the shrine of St David, and in the centre is the altar-tomb of Edmund Tudor, Earl of Richmond (died 1456), who was father of Henry VII. To the right lie Bishop Gervase (or Iorworth), 1229, and Anselm de la Grace, 1247. Near the middle of the chancel is the supposed tomb, bearing an effigy in armour, of Rhys ap Gruffydd, Lord Prince of South Wales (1197), the first Welsh prince to be interred in a Norman cathedral. There are many other tombs in the cathedral, including that, it is said, of the man who tried hard but failed to become its bishop—Giraldus Cambrensis.

The reader must arm himself with the booklet on sale inside the cathedral, for fuller details of the history of the building and its ancillary chapels. The cathedral is being restored by degrees in its more crumbling ancient parts. After a tour of this loveliest and most venerable of churches in Wales, he will be a rare misanthrope who will not gladly contribute to the collection box at the door.

Outside, the north wall of the nave of this instable cathedral was supported in the sixteenth century by powerful flying buttresses. Nearby are the imposing remains of St Mary's College,

8   113

Memorial to commemorate the last invasion of Britain, by the French in 1797, near Fishguard

founded for secular canons in 1365 by Bishop Houghton. The ancient wall of the cathedral close is seen to embrace a fair acreage of the valley, with the old precentory (now the Deanery) in the south-west corner, the ruined bishop's palace close to the river, and in the north-east the houses, or sites of houses, of the archdeacons of St David's, Brecon and Cardigan, and of the chancellor and the treasurer. The cathedral tower has a clock, but the bells are rung in an ancient octagonal gate tower with portcullis which stands in the south-east wall, over the main entrance to the cathedral close; probably they were transferred to this site when the cathedral belfry collapsed in 1220.

The lovely substantial ruins of the bishops' palace at St David's consist of three ranges of buildings covering the west, east and south sides of a square, entered by a vaulted gateway in the north wall. There, on the left of the great courtyard as one stands upon the smooth mown grass inside the gate, is the bishops' chapel, solar and hall, which are carried on a series of barrel vaults along the south of the palace. A substantial kitchen is strategically situated between the bishops' hall and the great hall itself. This great hall is 119 feet by 31 feet, approached by stairs from the courtyard, and its walls are crowned with the arcaded parapet finely built by skilled craftsmen under Bishop Gower, the main instigator and inspiration of the present building. It was used for the entertainment of the important guests which were in his time (1327–47) flocking to the shrine of the Welsh saint as if to Rome. The rose window is an exquisite touch to a palace which must have been one of the finest of such buildings in the country.

From cathedral and bishops' palaces we can look back upon the other Norman buildings in Pembrokeshire which, erected contemporaneously, survive for our pleasure today. The oldest—Pembroke, Cilgerran and Newport castles—go back for their beginnings to William I, who in 1081 with his armed following visited St David's and was entertained there by the Welsh bishop Sulien. Four years previously the internecine battles between the Welsh princes were at the point when Rhys ap Tewdwr had conquered and settled south Wales. He retired discreetly before this Norman visit; but in 1093 he arrived from Ireland and routed the Norman invaders in battles near the Teify river in north Pembrokeshire. This delayed the building there of the castle of Cilgerran, begun in 1092, by Roger Montgomery (who had led the right wing of the Norman army at the battle of Hastings).

Meanwhile in 1090 Roger's son Arnulph had landed at Pembroke and thrown up the earth and palisade fort which was to become the main Norman base in west Wales. Then in 1094 Martin de Turribus landed at Fishguard and laid the foundation of the Norman lord marchership of Cemaes, as described earlier in this book.

The Welsh fought valiantly. They made an attack on Pembroke in 1092, and contained the garrison, under Gerald de Windsor, late Castellan of Windsor, in a state of siege. The story is told of how Gerald, when the last pigs were due for slaughter, instead of rationing them out to last as long as possible, had them cut up and thrown over the walls, to trick the Welsh into believing that there was plenty of food within. He then arranged for a letter to his liege lord Arnulph de Montgomery to be put in the way of being picked up by the enemy: in this letter he stated that he needed neither reinforcements nor stores for four months. This ruse finally convinced the impatient Welsh and they departed.

Arnulph turned traitor to Henry I and with his brother Belesme from Cilgerran made peace with the Welsh under Grufudd, son of Rhys ap Tewdwr. He sent Gerald de Windsor to Ireland to raise troops there. This mixed army of Welsh, Irish and Norman followers was defeated at Shrewsbury by Henry, who banished Belesme and Arnulph.

Gerald de Windsor in the moment of co-operation with the Welsh had married Nesta, the fabulously beautiful daughter of Prince Rhys. Henry deprived him of his castellanship of Pembroke and Nesta was for a time the mistress of the King. Probably because of his love for Nesta the King restored Gerald as castellan of Pembroke, to be held for the King; and Carew and Manorbier were given as Nesta's dowry. Gerald built these two castles during these years when he lived peaceably in Wales.

In 1108 Cadwgan ap Blethyn, Prince of Powis, held a grand eisteddfod at Cardigan. Bards sang of the wondrous beauty of the

Welsh princess Nesta and she was likened to Helen of Troy. The adventurous young Owain, son of Cadwgan, thereupon planned to abduct this fair woman out of the bed of the Norman castellan. He rode to Pembroke (some say Carew) Castle, where he claimed kinship with Nesta through her father, the late Prince Rhys ap Tewdwr, and was admitted by Gerald de Windsor as an honoured guest. At the end of his visit Owain left the castle, only to return secretly at night with his men. He took prisoner Nesta and her two small sons as well as two illegitimate children of Gerald.

Henry banished both Cadwgan and his son Owain. The hasty young Owain, on his way to meet Henry and ask his forgiveness, encountered a Flemish bishop, one of Henry's recent importations, and incontinently murdered the prelate. This decided the King to remove the too easy-going Gerald from Pembroke and install Gilbert de Clare, a Norman warrior who forthwith attacked the Welsh, overran Cardiganshire, and built the castles of Cardigan, Aberystwyth and Haverfordwest. He also renovated Cilgerran castle.

Gilbert became Earl of Pembroke, and his son, Strongbow, attacked and conquered Ireland from Pembroke.

The lovely Nesta, having been the mistress of Henry I, wife of Gerald de Windsor, and seduced by Owain (by all three men she apparently had children), was to become the wife of Stephen, castellan of Cardigan. From her several liaisons came the famous families of Fitzgerald, de Barri, Geraldine, Carew and Carey. One of her sons, by Gerald de Windsor, became Bishop of St David's.

Henry gave Pembroke a special charter as a palatinate town, which enabled its Earl to have almost viceregal powers. Henry VII was born in Pembroke Castle. Henry VIII abolished the palatinate.

The descendants of Nesta, her sons and their retainers, were involved in the conquest of Ireland from Pembrokeshire. Many noble, ignoble and bloody adventures are recorded in Laws' book, in which the Pembrokeshire men fought, killed and were killed by native Irish and by Scandinavian-Irish chieftains and their retainers (the "kings" of Dublin and other Irish settlements were often Norsemen). Some south Irish place-names today are the same as some in Pembrokeshire, as a result of Strongbow's Irish campaign and acquisition of Irish lands, to which his Pembrokeshire soldier-squires gave their names on settling in Ireland.

Carew Castle, built by Gerald de Windsor for his wife Nesta, was altered and improved to become one of the most beautiful residential castles in Wales, with a great banqueting hall having wide freestone windows overlooking the present tide-water mill pond. It is still the property of Nesta's descendants, the Trollope-Bellew family. At one time it fell into the hands of the Welsh noble Rhys ap Thomas, the man who had declared in a letter to King Richard of England that no enemy would enter west Wales except "over my bellie". When Henry Richmond landed at Dale in 1485 Rhys went to meet him, and it is said that to fulfil the boast he lay down so that Henry could step across his body. He accompanied Henry to meet Richard's forces at Bosworth Field, when Rhys's men helped to win the day for Henry, who was crowned with the crown which had fallen from Richard's head. The new king knighted Rhys forthwith. On his veteran battle horse "Grey Fetterlocks" the Lord of Carew took part in other expeditions for Henry, who suitably rewarded him with honours and lordships.

In 1507 Sir Rhys held a princely tournament at Carew. The castle was packed full with distinguished guests, who overflowed into tents and pavilions on the green plain round about. Two hundred retainers wearing blue livery attended Sir Rhys. At the feast a chair was placed under a crimson canopy for the King, and meat for His Majesty as if he were there. There was jousting and games, but no one was seriously hurt. Sir Rhys would not permit quarrels or unjust words, and placed men with staves to strike up swords which were too much in earnest. A ceremonial visit was paid to the Bishop of St David's at nearby Lamphey Palace; and after mass the Bishop and his friends were brought to Carew to dinner. There was a deer hunt in the park and several buck were killed and sent to Carmarthen, where Griffith, the illegitimate son of Sir Rhys, was to give a farewell supper as a result of losing the last tilting match.

The present (remains of) beautiful mullioned windows are the work of the Elizabethan, Sir John Perrot, who was the last to make extensive additions. The castle was taken in 1644 by the Parliamentarians and did not remain habitable for much longer.

Lamphey Palace, often mentioned in this book, is well worth half a day of exploration. Here rusticated in ease among the Norman gentry the Bishops of St David's. The chapel where Sir Rhys heard mass on the occasion of his great tournament has a beautiful east window, probably by Bishop Gower (1328-47). When Bishop Rawlins died at Lamphey in 1536 his possessions included "a parliament robe of scarlet eaten with a rat in the back, and perished with moths, 40s." Obviously the Bishop had not been a frequent visitor to the House of Lords.

Henry VIII sold the Palace to Walter Devereaux, ancestor of Queen Elizabeth's favourite Robert Earl of Essex, who as a child lived at Lamphey. The Owen family of Orielton bought Lamphey from the Essex ownership, but in 1811 sold it to the Mathias family, still in possession.

Manorbier is the next nearest castle in south Pembrokeshire; already described as the home of Gerald, her historian. As it stands today it is small but noble-looking on its eminence commanding the sea bay. A gatehouse covers the land approach. The inner ward has a curtain-wall, there is a chapel and solar: all of which are open to public inspection during the summer.

Upton Castle lies secluded on the peninsula of Cosheston, looking out upon the broad tidal water of the Carew river. It belonged to the Malefant family (thirteenth century). Only the entrance gate with towers appears to have survived of the Norman building, but the separate chapel contains some of the oldest effigies in the country, of unknown characters. At present it is the home of the Neales, a trawler-owning family, and the grounds are remarkable for a collection of unusual shrubs, rhododendrons and trees.

Narberth Castle is associated with the legends of the Mabinogion, which tell of the Prince of Dyfed, Pwyll, whose city was Arberth. Strange adventures overtake this prince when he goes stag-hunting over the Prescelly Mountains and encounters the hounds of Hell under the King Annwvyn thereof (Satan). He agrees to change places with the King of Hell for a year. He completes his bargain steadfastly, and after many trials he is united to the beautiful Rhiannon and lives happily at Arberth until he died. Their son Pryderi had as strange adventures and it is said rested for eighty years on the island of "Gwalas in Penvro" (Grassholm in Pembrokeshire), "a fair and regal spot overlooking ocean, and a spacious hall was therein".

Narberth Castle was built about 1246 by Sir Andrew Perrot. Henry VIII made it over to Sir Rhys, who put it in order. It has been but a poor ruin for probably 250 years.

Amroth Castle, today a private guest-house, is a modern building on an old foundation. Nearby is Hean Castle, still newer, the home of Lord Merthyr.

Leaving the coast and proceeding by the road towards Haverfordwest, we pass Llawhaden Castle, the bishop's stronghold, and a few miles westwards lies the ruins of Wiston Castle, now a mere circular stone tower, tumbling on its mound in the centre of an earthen ring or rampart, which in its day of Norman pride was no doubt a heavily stockaded fence. Laws records that it may have been the scene of many bloody battles.

South of Wiston, by the side of the salt river of the East Cleddau, is Slebech, a manor house rather than a castle. It has recently been reconditioned by the Philipps family, but is not a very old building. Slebech is memorable as the site of a commandery of the famous knights of St John of Jerusalem or Malta, only the little church of which survives, with many interesting old memorials and recumbent figures. It is said that this was once the village church but the owner of Slebech desiring to keep the historic building as a family chapel, built the be-spired but uninspiring church by the main Carmarthen-Haverfordwest road to placate the parishioners.

Slebech Hall was the home of the Barlow family under Roger Barlow, a vice-admiral stationed at Milford Haven (in the time of Henry VIII) who bought the great estate of Slebech for £205 6s. In the knights' church lie buried Sir William Hamilton, already referred to in the chapter on Milford Haven, and his first wife, a Barlow heiress, whom at first he despised—having married for money—but after living with the beautiful but shameless Emma (the mistress of Charles Greville and of Nelson) his second, he left instructions for his burial beside his first.

Picton Castle, farther west above the Cleddau river, was begun by William de Picton, the Norman follower of Arnulph de Montgomery, and, frequently altered and modernised, has been inhabited ever since by descendants of Picton, although the male line has become extinct from time to time. The present holder is the Hon. Hanning Philipps.

Haverfordwest Castle stands magnificently on a crag above the town. It was begun by Gilbert de Clare and may have been completed by William de Valence in the thirteenth century. It is noted as withstanding the falcon-like swoops of the Welsh, including a siege by Owain Glyndwr's French contingents in 1405, who laid the town waste. Cromwell drove the King's garrison from this castle in 1644 and in 1648 it was ordered to be demolished. The solid walls resisted demolition, the inside alone was gutted. Latterly it was used as a prison; part of the castle now forms the new County Museum (1967).

Roche Castle, on an inland rock commanding the centre of St Bride's Bay, was an outpost against the Welsh inhabiting the northward hills and bogs. It is a small Peel tower castle of Henry III date, and at one time was the home of Lucy Walters, mistress of Charles II. It has been inhabited almost continuously, and has lately passed out of the possession of Lord St Davids who had modernised the interior.

Dale Castle, in the south-west peninsula of the rural district of Haverfordwest, was anciently the home of the Norman de Vale family, who also possessed the islands of Skomer and Skokholm, the latter still owned by the present owner of the modern Dale Castle, Hugh Lloyd-Philipps Esqre. Dale, with its tall-towered church, lies prettily in the vale of the isthmus but as already mentioned modern houses have destroyed some of its charm.

Not far away, occupying a similar position on the neck of an isthmus, is St Brides, a bay having only a church, rectory and two cottages near its open harbour and beach. This is a lovely spot, sheltered from the south, but open to the northerly gales.

Beside the church are the extensive ivy-clad and tree-covered ruins of a vast mansion and grounds. These were the possession of John de St Bride, a follower of Henry III. In Fenton's time it was a ruin and the owner, Charles Philipps, had built the present Castle of St Brides, on the hill to the west. This two-hundred-year-old house is now known as Kensington Hospital (from the late Lord Kensington who owned St Brides), a convalescent home for tubercular children. St Brides was formerly the site of a local herring fishery: a chapel stood on its shore, but

> "When St Bride's chapel a salt house was made
> St Bride's lost the herring trade."

More than that, the sea swept in and devoured the chapel and much of its graveyard, so that even today the odd gravestone is seen peering out of the eroded shore, near an ancient lime-kiln.

If we search about we find yet a few more castles and old manors in the southern part of Pembrokeshire. There is Benton, lying in the woods on the western bank of the Cleddau overlooking Castle Reach, so-called after Benton castle. About the same period as Roche, and with the same late Norman Peel tower, it was uninhabited from the time of its reduction by Cromwell until about 1930 when its reconstruction was undertaken by a genial hermit Ernest Pegge, who with his own hands lovingly rebuilt it, using the rock tumbled from its walls by time and Cromwellian cannons, and oak beams from the shipbreakers' yards at Milford Haven. Many a happy hour have I spent with Ernest Pegge, a surprising but sane man and contented as he worked in and about his castle in the lovely wooded, estuarine environment. He placed his own mask, in concrete, over the entrance to the renovated castle. The woods all along this western shore, where sheld-duck nest in old tree hollows and holes, and badgers and foxes roam, and red squirrels play, are dedicated to the Forestry Commission and will remain as Pegge wished, a perfect sanctuary for natural life.

To enumerate and sketch even briefly the history of manors and "strong" houses in the south of the county would fill another book, with anecdotes of Norman and Medieval days. Such houses

—of a meaner size—were also scattered in the wild Welsh northern half of the county, where the main Norman outposts were Newport, Cardigan and Cilgerran castles.

Most striking of these is Cilgerran, rising above the dark canyon walls of the Teify river, in the heart of the Welsh part of west Wales. Roger de Belesme began this castle about the year 1092, but the Norman adventurers were repulsed many times. It was rebuilt about 1223. In the interval it was occupied for long periods by the Welsh, who withstood many a siege by the English. The romantic spirit of the great King Arthur is associated with Cilgerran, the name is said to mean "the cell of Geraint", a Round Table Knight. Only the shell of two of the main towers remains. The castle was built of the local slate stone, cemented together with the tenacious mortar used by Norman masons. It is now the property of the National Trust. Turner and Richard Wilson painted it. In the nearby churchyard is an inscribed (Ogam-Latin) stone.

Along the Teify here lie Llechryd and Cenarth, where men fish in round dish-like coracles, made of osier and canvas (formerly osier and hide), and catch rather too many of the fine Teify salmon and sewin (sea-trout) for the liking of the gentlemen rod-fishers. Bnt we hope that the coracle men will not be selfishly driven from the river which is their most ancient heritage by the plan (to refuse licences to their sons and successors) devised by the Fisheries Board. Long may the picturesque coracle float downstream, and be carried upstream on the backs of skilful Welsh fishermen.

A tributary of the Teify is the Cych, whose sycamores are mentioned in the *Mabinogion*. At Abercych a wood-turnery flourishes, begun centuries ago with hand-tools, and now producing substantial parcels of broom-handles, wooden rakes, staves and axe-handles, and in one or two houses utensils are still hand-made.

All this northern hinterland of Pembrokeshire is a grand place for quiet exploration.

CHAPTER **X**

MODERN TIMES

THE population of Pembrokeshire in 1801 was 56,280. In sixty years it had nearly doubled: 96,278, its highest ever recorded. This was the peak of the shipbuilding boom in Milford Haven. From Haverfordwest along the creeks southwards to the main yards of Pembroke Dock and Milford Dock the skilled work of shipwrighting went on. The anthracite mines employed up to 600 men, and the limestone quarries, the lead mines and slate quarries, the woollen mills, the agricultural industry (corn exports included) were flourishing. This period is sometimes called the Golden Age of Agriculture. The day of universal mechanised road transport and of steam navigation was at hand, however, and after the peak came a steady decline until by 1931, following the closure of the Naval Base at Pembroke Dock, the county population was reduced by 10,000. It has not recovered much since: War Department seizure of 10 square miles of the best farming land in the limestone area of Castlemartin in 1939 has not helped. With the appearance of the Coal Board the last of the anthracite mines were closed. Small factories at Pembroke Dock, which experience changeable fortune, manage to retain a limited proportion of the Borough's former industrial workers. But primarily Pembrokeshire has gone back to its dependence on agriculture, with today, to a minor extent, the deepsea trawling, oil refineries and summer visitors as auxiliary industries.

The last, attracted more and more by the appeal and publicity given to the new National Coast Park of Pembrokeshire, is becoming a not unimportant seasonal source of revenue. In connection with this Park and all it may bring for the future, the importance of the comprehensive development plan for the county, finally prepared by Mr J. A. Price, the Planning Officer, in 1953, is very evident. The whole of the county has now been surveyed under the Planning Acts and the result—a document of over

200 foolscap pages—reflects great credit both on the County Council and Mr Price. The proper management of this great estate is now a principal concern of the County Planning Committee. This has recognised the advantages of maintaining the "outstanding scenic beauty of Pembrokeshire which could be spoiled by ill-conceived development. It is essential that a means of protecting this heritage should be adopted, and that action be taken immediately to remove the unfortunate evidence of wartime activities".

It is a considerable responsibility to call the attention of the world to an area of such unspoilt wildness and beauty, and then both to encourage visitors to it and at the same time defend it from spoliation by those visitors. Compared with the great national parks of the New World and Africa, for example, the Pembrokeshire Park is but a small area and easily spoiled by careless relaxation of planning controls. Alas, as I write this, the "march of progress" continues, business interests have encouraged industry to settle along Milford Haven, even within the National Park, while new W.D. buildings and establishments continue to encroach both on the north and the south coasts of the county. These, and the too facile granting of coast development for holiday houses, caravans and car parks, are a direct reproach to the declared policy written into the Committee's report.

In this report, by contrast, is an illuminating description of the isolated village of Landshipping, almost as deserted as Goldsmith's sweet Auburn, which I quote by kind permission of Mr Price and the Pembrokeshire County Council.

"It was left to its own devices when the coal mining industry left the area, and has steadily declined ever since from a more or less busy area, to a quiet neglected backwater with few of the amenities of modern existence.

"Cottages that housed miners and surface workers and houses that accommodated officials, as well as shops and public houses, have long since disappeared, and the only evidence that Landshipping was once a busy place are the ruined quays on the riverside and the scarred surface and slag heaps that disfigure the area and make the resident industry, farming, more than ordinarily difficult.

"In more prosperous times Landshipping was linked with Haverfordwest by water traffic and by road crossing Landshipping Ferry. The abandoning of the coal mines was followed by the decline of traffic over the Ferry and it is some years now since the Ferry was last operated and a bus service was available on the Picton side to take people to Haverfordwest for marketing and for shopping. To all intents and purposes, the present village, if village it can be called, for it is scattered over a wide area and has no point of focus unless it be the village pub, is cut off from the rest of the world. It is at the dead end of a road that once was carried on over the Ferry, but which now finishes abruptly at the river's edge, and those who would continue their journey must retrace their footsteps to Crosshands or Martletwy. A journey to Haverfordwest, distance about five miles as the crow flies, means a detour over Canaston Bridge involving a distance of some fourteen miles. The distance to Pembroke and Pembroke Dock is similarly extended by the contortions of the Cleddau and the lack of bridges, which no doubt are impracticable over the wide and muddy creeks connecting with the river.

"The nearest provision shop and that but a small one, is situated two miles away in the village of Martletwy, with no means of getting there but by walking. For shopping in other than the most primitive requirements, villagers must visit Narberth, to reach which they walk a half-mile or so to catch the one and only bus in the week, at Clare House corner, and pay half a crown for the return journey—for some obscure reason, sixpence more than the cost of the return journey *from* Narberth, by the same bus! (But it would not be possible in the latter case to return the same day.)

"Now the fact is that few villagers are able to effect their shopping in this way, and so it happens that most foodstuffs and many minor household items are brought to the village by travelling salesmen. Needless to say, though in the circumstances convenient, this does not prove very satisfactory, for travelling salesmen are not able to offer any but the narrowest if any choice of goods. Moreover, in bad weather it is not unknown for baker, butcher, and grocer to fail to put in an appearance. The desire for a wider selection of goods is met to some extent by the Mail Order houses, who do a very considerable trade in the village. There is no doctor available nearer than Martletwy Village, where a Narberth practitioner holds surgery weekly on Mondays; and on the same afternoon visits patients in the village. At any other time a doctor cannot be got nearer than Narberth.

"It will be observed that almost every answer given to the questionnaire is in the negative. There is no village Church or Chapel or School, no village Hall, no railway within five miles, no shops, no recreation grounds, no sporting activities, no bus service, no electricity, and, apart from a number of very doubt-ful wells, no water. It is, in fact, appalling that such a state of affairs should be allowed to persist. It is a sorry sight in this weather to see the children trapesing through the wet every morning to attend school at Martletwy. Villagers say among themselves that were one of these a child of some Councillor or pampered official, it would not be in vain that they would look for a school bus service.

"Electric cables (the grid) run 'through' the village; yet no one is able to get a supply of electricity. A water scheme has been sanctioned and a contract actually given out; but no one is interested in getting the work started: and so the villagers continue to drink water that in some cases would probably be refused by townspeople even for washing purposes. There is much worse that might be said about this neglected corner of Pembrokeshire, but this is hardly the occasion to do so. Let it not be thought, however, that Landshipping is not a happy village; it is! very happy!! Those who cannot surmount the difficulties—leave; those who are left find pleasure in helping one another out. It is significant that wireless entertainment counts for little—probably because of the lack of electricity and the high cost of batteries."

However, at least the post comes daily, and the milk lorry, both modern lines of communication which the astute country-man well knows how to make use of!

To the naturalist and country-lover Landshipping is neverthe-less a remote and lovely part, and we are not altogether surprised to learn that its inhabitants are very happy!

There are few other parishes in Pembrokeshire quite so isolated, but some of the northern hill villages like Llys-y-fran, Llanfyrnach, Mynachlogddu, Morvil, Meline, dream delight-fully in their agricultural wilderness without recent develop-ment—and long may they do so in this modern world of over-industrialisation.

To some of the remote communities buses now come to collect and return each day the sons and daughters (of countrymen engaged in farming and rural tasks) to work in government establishments; and this has brought some taxpayers' money back to the land, at least temporarily. Some of this is saved to put into the farm, some goes into television sets, motor vehicles, and enter-tainment.

The Forestry Commission has appeared in the county and has taken over the old woodland of Canaston, some three thousand acres in the centre of the county, and has built a model forest hamlet near the old watermill at Black Pool—to which no longer come the wooden ketches and sailing barges at high water of spring tides. Instead, like the new saplings rising in these old hunting groves of Welsh princes and Norman lords and Victorian squires, new life is rising Phoenix-like over the ashes of the old in Pembrokeshire, with state-paid foresters residing in comfortable attractive modern houses, albeit paid for out of the taxpayers' pocket.

There are, surprisingly, nearly ten thousand acres of existing woodland in Pembrokeshire, much of it hidden away from the Atlantic gales in deep *cwms* and sheltered valleys. Of this total about 3,500 is high mature forest, but on the whole indifferently managed. The rest is hardly better than scrub, having been felled during the last two world wars, and neglected since. The Forestry Commission is trying to remedy this sorry state of affairs and by grants and advice to private owners of woodlands reafforestation is gradually making progress.

Next to Flintshire, Pembrokeshire is classed as the most fertile county in Wales (Table 30 of the National Farm Survey of England and Wales) having 14 per cent good, 67 per cent medium, and 19 per cent poor quality land, of its 392,300 agricultural acres. Margaret F. Davies in her report on Pembrokeshire (*Land Utilisation Survey of Britain*, 1939) extracts the following statistics on land use in the county:

Land Utilisation	Pembrokeshire Per cent	Wales Per cent
Arable	20	13
Meadow and Permanent Grass	51	42
Moorland and Rough Grazing	17	32
Woods	2	4
Miscellaneous	10	9

The last war caused a sharp rise to about 35 per cent of land under the plough (1949), but once more fields are being laid down to pasture at a rapid rate as corn becomes less and less profitable, with a wheat surplus embarrassing the world market.

Oats are the most popular crop, up to 40 thousand acres are grown annually; early potatoes come next, about eight thousand (about ten thousand with maincrops) acres; barley for seed, malting or home consumption, about eight thousand acres; wheat barely reaches two thousand, and sugar-beet 1,400 acres.

As to the sea fishery, Milford Haven trawlers now land about 5–6 per cent of the wet fish (chiefly hake) of the national catch. The port had the fifth largest fleet in the kingdom in 1950, with ninety-seven first-class registered sea-fishing boats, of which all but eight were steam navigated. In 1950 the value of the fish landed was £1,642,080.

The inshore fishery is not in such a good state: it has declined steadily, and although many small open boats are registered for fishing, the number actually used for full-time catching of crabs, lobster, crayfish, herring, mackerel, whiting, pollack and salmon

Upton Castle, one of the few still inhabited of many castles built by the Normans against the Welsh native population, which retreated to the northern hills and harried the invaders for several hundred years

is low, well under fifty out of a registered total of over one hundred boats (1951). This decline I would put down (as a once full-time inshore fisherman) to excessive exploitation of the inshore grounds by a few fishermen in powerful three-man crew motor boats, to poaching (often at night) by trawlers within the three-mile limit, and to oil pollution. I do not agree that the large numbers of sea-birds (gannets, cormorants and shags) or of seals and porpoises alleged to prey disastrously upon these fish in Pembrokeshire waters, have had more than a limited effect. Fishermen have always waged war on these ancient rivals of theirs, although lately some boatmen have found it convenient to preserve them because of the interest shown by tourists and summer visitors. At St David's, Dale, Martinshaven, Milford and Tenby fishermen now regularly hire their boats for "sea-bird" trips to the outer islands and coasts.

Water supplies in Pembrokeshire usually fall all too freely from the sky, but rainfall is low in the coast areas, especially in the south-west (35 inches per annum) where no mains supply is yet laid on to the hamlets and farms. There are local reservoirs serving villages and farms, but many cottages and some farms have no piped indoor supply.

There is only one reservoir of any size in Pembrokeshire. This was built by the Milford Haven Urban Council at Rosebush, where the great bowl of the catchment area (65 inches of rain per annum) of 2,050 acres south-west of the highest point of the Prescelly Mountains converges at the waterfall of Afon Syfynwy. This reservoir was completed in 1932 and held 75 million gallons. When Tenby Borough and Narberth Rural District required a supply, the dam was raised 10 feet, enabling 170 million gallons to be impounded. Further raising of the dam is contemplated to make it possible to supply yet more of the water needs of people, farms and industry in Pembrokeshire.

Main electricity and gas supplies and sewerage are, as might be expected in a remote county far from the industrial and population centres of Britain, not universal, although the Electricity Board supply reaches the main towns and large villages.

Re-housing progresses slowly. To the visitor who does not

A herd of Atlantic grey seals lying out on a remote beach. The bulls are darker in coat than the cow seals have to live in them, the little stone-built, mortar-covered, colour-washed cottages characteristic of many of the country lanes and villages, are pleasing by their age and colour. Inside they are very cramped, dark and inconvenient, having often only two main rooms and a lean-to at the back, with no bathroom or indoor closet. They are terribly drab when strung together, undetached and not colour-washed, as for example at Pembroke Dock. There the cottages were built of red brick which was not durable and had to be dashed over with concrete. Also at Milford Haven, Haverfordwest and Tenby, where they were run up about a hundred years or so ago by landlords, in the industrial boom of that period. If only these rows of dwarf cottages could be kept exteriorly washed in different shades of cream, white, pink, blue, etc., they would today be picturesque, though classed as slums. The streets of Pembroke and Pembroke Dock would then be quite pleasant to pass through, instead of being, as they now often are, offensive to the eye.

The "Long House" (a proper name still given to a few farms) farmhouse with byre and barn all in one long rectangular building, with thick walls of stone and mud mortared over, is still commonly seen, some derelict, but many occupied. This is the oldest surviving type of Welsh farmhouse, the home of the wealthier farmer, descendant of the men of the *gwelys* and the chieftains, the *uchelwyr*. Pembrokeshire houses were formerly thatched, but with the opening of slate quarries in Wales, including Pembrokeshire, slate roofing became popular because of its durability. Small soft slates of a delicate deep blue were quarried at Rosebush until recently; they cover many Pembrokeshire homes today. These were laid on the roof with oak pegs fixed in a hole drilled at the top of each slate, being merely hooked by this peg over thin split battens nailed to the rafters. The finished roof was rendered underneath with lime mortar which cemented peg and batten and slate in a white under-sheet, which also kept out the wind. In the course of a hundred years or so the pegs and battens tended to decay: at the first sign of the loosening of the roof the mason would be called in to "grout" (that is, to brush a thin coat of mortar, or latterly sand and cement) over the exterior of the roof. This is but a temporary expedient, for the sealed roof can no longer "breathe", and rot is merely accelerated. The next stage, to prevent the whole roof of slates sliding down over the eaves, is to pass wires from one eave over the ridge to the other eave, and grout these bonds into the already heavily grouted roof. Annual grouting of the slates is the final stage, staving off the day when either the roof collapses, or is dismantled and replaced altogether.

The earliest houses, if not of stone, had mud and straw walls, "daub and wattle" or a compound known in English as "cob". But the abundance of loose stone in Pembrokeshire led to the replacement of straw with stone. Mud was still used, as an interior mortar. When a mud-cemented stone wall was completed it was washed exteriorly with water until the stone was clean: then a strong mortar of lime, ashes and sand was dashed on the outside to render the wall moisture-impervious. The house and buildings on Skokholm Island, for example, were built in this fashion, as I found when repairing them. Nevertheless they had withstood many a 100-m.p.h. gale during their centuries-old existence.

Castles and fortified houses were built on a stronger plan, with mortar inside and out. The Norman influence is plain in many an existing farmhouse today: thick walls go with deep-recessed doors and windows, arched entrances and stone and slate slab stairways and benches. The so-called round Flemish chimneys of some of the older houses generally carried away the smoke from the large bread-ovens which up to 1900 were a feature of every farmhouse and many cottages. In these ovens large wood fires were lit, and when burnt out the ash was raked away; the lumps of dough and perhaps the weekly joint of meat were thrust in with a special shovel, the iron door was shut and the hot oven sealed with wet clay. The conservation of moisture in bread and meat in the sealed hot oven resulted in perfect cooking a few hours later.

So long as the little anthracite mines were worked in Pembrokeshire, the dust and grit from the coal face provided an abundant supply of cheap firing for the inhabitants of the county. This dust, mixed with an equal part of local clay, and watered, formed "culm", a slow-burning, highly economical fuel. It was rolled into small balls by the thrifty farmwife, and laid to burn in neat rows in the basket grate which at one time was universal in Pembrokeshire. These open grates or stoves heated a water tank on the left side, and an oven upon the right side, with a large open chimney to carry the smokeless fumes aloft. Many farmwives and cottagers claim that their culm fires have never gone out in twenty years or so. Owing to the difficulty of starting these slow-burning fires, it was the practice to "stum" (bank-up) the top of the fire each night with a shovelful of wet culm; a hole was made in the centre of the wet culm, and through this the blue flame lived the night long.

Modern ranges and electric fires are displacing the old culm fires, although anthracite dust is still imported into Pembrokeshire from nearby Carmarthenshire collieries.

As to roads, Pembrokeshire is sufficiently supplied not to want any extensive improvements to these, although it is to be feared that others think otherwise, especially the ardent motorist. Nevertheless, in our humble opinion, it is a grave mistake to broaden and straighten Pembrokeshire's pleasant roads.

CHAPTER XI

FOR THE NATURALIST

THE combination of mountain and sea, of bare moorland and wooded valley, of fertile farmland and bleak stone-scattered cliff, of sandy bay and sheltered haven, and the rocky wave-beaten islands, provide a rich diversity of country for the naturalist—although on account of the distance of Pembrokeshire from the larger centres of population it is comparatively little explored.

The ornithologist will find that the number of species of birds recorded in the county, nearly 300, exceeds that of any other county in Wales, even of Glamorgan, which has always had the largest number of observers. Examining the lists for the twelve Welsh counties one notices that Pembrokeshire has a rather larger number of resident breeding species and a somewhat smaller number of summer-visiting breeding species. The main difference, however, is in the large number of regular and occasional visitors, due to the position of the county lying in the path of the west coast migration of birds each spring and autumn, as well as to the number of rare or very rare birds recorded at Skokholm Island since the work of the Island Observatory began in 1933. Some of these rarities have never been recorded elsewhere in Wales.

Wild mammals are few in species, but plentiful by numbers. The largest British wild mammal, the Atlantic grey seal, is numerous along the coast, and may be seen swimming close inshore or basking on the rocks at low tide. Probably some 400 grey seal calves are born each autumn on Pembrokeshire beaches, especially those in caves and coves on the islands of Ramsey and Skomer, and under the high wild cliffs of the mainland. Members of the West Wales Naturalists' Trust have recently ring-marked each year about a quarter (100) of the more accessible of these calves, with interesting results: some have swum far within a few weeks of birth, being reported from southern Ireland, Cornwall and

Britanny, one even from Northern Spain. The other British seal, the common seal, numerous in the North Sea, has rarely been certainly identified in Pembrokeshire waters.

Deer are no longer found in the county, although there are unconfirmed reports of roe-deer reaching the wooded eastern edge, it is suggested as a result of the reafforestation taking place in counties to the east. Fallow deer existed in many parks in Pembrokeshire in Elizabethan times and probably the last were killed at Lawrenny Park shortly before 1939.

Foxes are present but not numerously—often the local hunts fail to find one. Undoubtedly the steel-toothed rabbit trap was responsible for the scarcity of foxes until myxomatosis in 1954 ended the rabbit trade and virtually put paid to this cruel trap. Since that year foxes have actually increased in Pembrokeshire, despite the shortage of rabbits, a fact which seems to prove that the fox is not dependent on the rabbit as a main article of diet.

Badgers are more numerous in Pembrokeshire than in any part of Britain that I know. Almost every small wood, copse, spinney or rough scrub-covered cliff has its badger's "sett". They are harmless creatures, slow-moving, ambling and shuffling along like miniature bears, subsisting principally on earthworms, small mammals, insects, roots and vegetation. They will eat a little ripe corn and may roll down patches of oats, barley or wheat to get at the ears. They are too slow to catch healthy adult rabbits, but freely dig out the shallow nests of the doe. At Orielton a colony established itself in the drains beneath the stables and shovelled out many tons of soil, causing the floors to sink several inches: the underground grunting and movements of the badgers could be heard as one stood in the stables above.

Badgers will roll over rabbit-traps, which are thereby sprung, catching only a handful of bristles; they can pull their limbs out of traps without breaking their tough bones in a way fox and stoat cannot do. Thus they have escaped the lethal effects of this trap on small mammals. But the stoat has been quite exterminated by this trap over most of Pembrokeshire of recent years; the abolition of the trap, now illegal, may enable this wandering mustelid to re-colonise the county.

The weasel, for the same reason, is not common, although, living principally on rats, mice and voles, it has survived everywhere in small numbers. These appeared to have declined since the 1954 epidemic of myxomatosis swept most of the rabbit population away, with a corresponding decline (it is believed) in the numbers of other small rodents, due to predatory birds and mammals feeding on these in lieu of rabbits.

The polecat is found breeding in Cardiganshire, and from time to time individuals stray into Pembrokeshire, especially in the mountain region and the Gwaun Valley. The marten used to be common, but has not been recorded during this century, although found in central and north Wales.

The otter is found on all rivers, large streams and lakes, and along the shore, although seldom seen. It is hunted by the local otter-hound pack. It is destructive of wildfowl at Orielton Decoy.

Since game preservation has virtually ceased in the county, the hare has vanished—it was also a victim of the steel-jawed trap and of poachers. A few have been recorded recently on the Carmarthenshire border and the Prescelly range. There has been some interest among land-owners in re-establishing it, now that the rabbit has become scarce, but with what success we cannot yet report.

Rabbits have been the curse of Pembrokeshire's agriculture for fifty years to the extent that by 1946 the export of wild rabbit meat exceeded that of the county's output of beef, mutton and pork put together, and the farmer had become the victim of a vast parasitic organisation built up by the rabbit-trapper and dealer. In 1954 rabbits were suddenly reduced to a fraction of their former numbers by myxomatosis, deliberately introduced by certain long-suffering farmers who, it is said, collected infective material from the centre of the first outbreaks in south-eastern England and thus hastened the advent of what is naturally a slow-travelling disease (in Britain the rabbits' natural flea is the principal vector). By 1956 the disease had swept through the county and died out, leaving a residue equal to about 1 per cent of the former high population, and these survivors (only a few of which have proved immune) have ever since been attacked by hungry birds and animals of prey, and by farmers whose obligation, under the Rabbit Clearance Order for Pembrokeshire (excluding Skokholm Island), is to control and exterminate them. No land-user who suffered under the attacks of the rabbit would wish to see its recolonisation, with all the attendant misery of trapping and of damage to agriculture and forestry.

Of small rodents, Pembrokeshire has the bank vole (*Clethrionomys glareolus*), common in lower wooded country, the field vole (*Microtus agrestis*), numerous in upland and open districts and on Ramsey Island, the water vole (*Arvicola amphibius*) by every stream and large pond, the house-mouse (*Mus musculus*), the field or wood mouse (*Apodemus sylvaticus*), and the brown rat (*Rattus norvegicus*). The black rat (*Rattus rattus rattus*) and the yellow-necked wood mouse (*Apodemus flavicollis*) may exist but do not seem to have been recorded recently.

On Skomer is a large insular race of the bank vole known to science as *Clethrionomys glareolus Skomerensis*. It is very tame when caught, and has been bred successfully in captivity.

The dormouse has not been recorded in a wild state in Pembrokeshire.

The red squirrel is found, though always in small numbers, in the principal woods, as at Benton, Lawrenny, Hook, Picton, Slebech, Canaston, Orielton, Cresselly, Colby, and in the north of the county. Unfortunately since 1948 a few grey squirrels have appeared from time to time, the advance guard of immigrants known to be colonising Wales from the east.

The hedgehog is common in certain localities, especially in the south, for example near Tenby and at Orielton, and it is reported from most of the parishes in the county, though it too has been a victim of the rabbit-trap, which must have reduced its numbers considerably.

The common shrew (*Sorex araneus*), pigmy shrew (*S. minutus*), water-shrew (*Neomys fodiens*) and mole (*Talpa europaea*) are numerous everywhere.

The county has a good supply of bats, of which those most often identified are the cave-loving Greater and Lesser Horse-shoe (*Rhinolophus ferrum-equinum* and *R. hipposideros*), the Pipistrelle

(*Pipistrellus pipistrellus*), the Long-eared (*Plecotus auritus*), and the Whiskered (*Myotis mystacinus*). Michael Blackmore also lists Natterer's bat (*M. nattereri*). Lesser horse-shoe bats inhabit the cellars at Orielton and on summer evenings hunt regularly through the large rooms and passages of the old house. Great horse-shoe bats hang in clusters in the limestone caves, including the great Wogan Cavern under Pembroke Castle.

Of reptiles, the adder or viper is common on heaths and gorse-covered commons and cliff slopes. The grass-snake is not so common, but is seen on the lower sheltered ground, especially near streams and water. Slow- or blind-worms are very common, and survive even on the windswept islands of Skokholm, Skomer, Caldey and Ramsey. The common lizard (*Lacerta vivipara*) is to be seen basking in the sun on warm days, and is present on Skomer (but not Skokholm), Caldey and Ramsey, and up to about 800 feet on the Prescelly Range.

The common frog and toad are as abundant as elsewhere in Wales, but the only newt known in Pembrokeshire appears to be the palmated newt (*Triturus helveticus*).

★　　★　　★　　★　　★

A brief word as to the fishes and other large marine animals. Nearly one hundred species of fish have been identified in Pembrokeshire waters within the three-mile limit. Of these the small boat and shore line fishermen commonly take dogfish (or tope), conger, whiting, pollack, coal-fish, wrasse, mackerel, mullet, dab, plaice, flounder and bass. The rivers yield salmon, sewin (sea-trout), brown trout and eels.

Cockles are abundant at Dale and Angle, within the haven. Mussels cluster around rocks and piers along the whole coast. Lobsters, crabs and crayfish (spiny lobster, locally known as "seegur") form a profitable fishery, still carried on from Tenby, Stackpole Quay, Angle, Dale, Marloes, St Bride's Bay (including Solva), St. David's, and along the north coast to Fishguard and Cardigan.

The up-river fishery at Langwym has already been described.

Basking-sharks are seen close offshore from mid-summer on-wards to late autumn. Porpoises and dolphins are numerous; occasionally the killer whale appears.

★   ★   ★   ★   ★

Pembrokeshire is a county of birds, and this book would hardly be complete without some description of these and of their considerable migrations visible from this western edge of Wales, of the sea-birds already mentioned, and of the distribution of the land-birds.

Most of the wilder type of country is found from Dowrog Moor at St David's eastwards and north-eastwards to the boundaries with Cardiganshire and Carmarthenshire. Interspersed with stretches of undulating farmland (good along the drier coastal belt, but often poor inland) there are wet furze-covered moors, marshes, and hanging woods, the haunt of fox, badger, and the last polecats. In these wild surroundings, so beautiful in summer, but often so empty and bleak in winter, buzzards and ravens are always to be seen in the air. The wet sedgy furze moors are rich in bird life in summer; here the Montagu's harrier, the merlin and the short-eared owl have frequently bred. Curlew, lapwing, snipe, mallard, cuckoo, linnet, reed-bunting, stonechat, and meadow-pipit are dominant nesting species in this environment. Willow-, sedge- and grasshopper-warblers occupy bush cover over the ditches and waterholes on these lower moors.

Higher up, on the bare grass of the hills, between 800 and 1,600 feet, on well-drained slopes where sheep, ponies and cattle graze, bird life is much scarcer; the meadow-pipit alone is numerous, sharing these windy contours with scattered pairs of sky-larks, ravens and carrion-crows, and more rarely merlin and buzzard. The very tops of the mountains are usually smooth and grassy with occasional outcrops of rock where wheatears breed, but this species is comparatively scarce. There is very little heather, and therefore no red grouse. The cuckoo, never an abundant species in the county, shuns the high ground, never ascending above the lower fringe of the mountain land, the dark green rim at 800 feet where bracken flourishes and where stunted white- and blackthorns grow. Here breed a very few pairs of whinchat, especially near wet springs and streams. This is the breeding limit of the magpie and wren. Where the contours are cut by streams, at the head of "cwms", a few rowans, whitethorns and birch provide sufficient shelter for ring-ouzels, but this species is principally a spring visitor to the county. This is suitable country for black-game, but the species has long been extinct here, though it bred in George Owen's time. The dipper and grey wagtail are at home in the music of the little waterfalls from these hill streams, and may nest at any point along their course, from the 800-foot line to within a few feet of sea-level. On the lower more level banks of the hurrying streams they meet with the somewhat scarce king-fisher and the heron.

As the streams descend, the sides of the valleys often fall precipitously, with rock faces to which cling sturdy sessile oak, birch, and rowan and other indigenous trees. These high narrow glens, whose marshy bottoms are filled with golden saxifrage, kingcups and orchids in April and May, contain nesting pairs of chaffinch, willow-warbler, wren, carrion-crow and buzzard.

Farther down the valley the trees are more luxuriant, although the slopes may still be too steep for easy felling operations, and in that case the ancient oakwoods may remain. These indigenous oak-hangers occur principally inland, near the borders of neigh-bouring counties, and are nowhere extensive. Where they are well grown they are the favourite haunt of the wood-warbler, one of the few species that lives exclusively within their narrow boun-daries. They would indeed be rather birdless if it were not for the margin of mixed wood and farmland above and below; and the combination of the whole provides suitable nesting ground for the carrion-crow, chaffinch, great, blue and coal-tits, chiffchaff, willow-warbler, wood-warbler, song-thrush, blackbird, robin, wren, tree-creeper, tawny owl, kestrel, buzzard, sparrow-hawk, and wood pigeon. There are a few pairs of the redstart, nuthatch, green and great spotted woodpeckers.

At the edge of these wooded valleys, on the fringe of the little fields of the small farms of the hill districts, the tree-pipit is a characteristic but by no means abundant bird. These fields are the breeding haunt of the curlew, whose sweet whistle mingles with the bell-like notes of the wood-lark. The song of the wood-lark is, in fact, more often heard than the bolder song of the sky-lark in these hilly pastures bordering the valley woods, and it is probable that in the foothills of the Prescelly Mountains the wood-lark is as plentiful as it is anywhere else in Britain.

There is too little planted woodland in the county to merit a special description of afforested land as an ecological unit. Coniferous plantations are rare. It is usual to find that the natural woods are felled and then allowed to regenerate as they may; silviculture being a much neglected art in Pembrokeshire, where it is generally believed that the strong winds and salt air are not favourable to the growth of good timber (which, it must be admitted, is only found in deep sheltered valleys). When felled the natural woods re-grow slowly, providing an interesting sequence of habitats for breeding birds. The newly felled land quickly fills with foxglove and willow-herb, bracken and bramble, mixed with the shoots from the tree-stumps; these conditions are ideal for whitethroat, blackbird, wren and nightjar. In a few years a rapid growth of elder, thorn and bramble invites the willow-warbler, garden-warbler, long-tailed and marsh-tit, song-thrush, dunnock and robin. And as the stools of the old trees thrust higher and higher their armies of small saplings the new copse is formed, and a suitable home provided for those species preferring thicker cover, including the chiffchaff, blackcap and bullfinch.

It is, however, impossible to fix an arbitrary line dividing one woodland ecological type from another, fascinating as this categorising is, since a mingling of types occurs more often than not. A group of old trees is frequently left standing in an otherwise clear-felled wood, and the bird population is modified or enriched by the presence of such lovers of tall trees as mistle-thrush, jay, magpie, carrion-crow, tree-creeper, tawny owl, even perhaps the scarce long-eared owl, and almost certainly by the buzzard.

The agricultural lands surrounding the woods and covering much of the land from fell to foreshore contain the most varied bird life of the mainland of Pembrokeshire. Carrion-crow, rook, jackdaw and magpie are extremely common, the jackdaw especially along the coastal fringe where cliffs provide safe and easy housing accommodation. Probably all four species have increased as a result of the increase in the arable acreage in the county, due to two major wars. It is common to see arable fields black with rooks and jackdaws during seed-time and harvest, while roosting flocks of up to one hundred of the carrion-crow or of the magpie are also common, out of the breeding season. Two species, common in England and eastern Wales, are, however, surprisingly scarce: the starling and house-sparrow, which are quite absent from some villages and small towns. Sparrows, however, increase with increasing poultry flocks.

Finches are numerous in the following order: chaffinch, linnet, greenfinch and goldfinch, the two latter being almost equal in numbers. In a few orchards the lesser redpoll breeds, but is otherwise only a winter visitor in small numbers with the siskin. The yellow bunting is probably the commonest small bird of open arable areas. The corn-bunting, once local, has lately vanished. The cirl bunting has bred, but the small colony near Solva appears to have died out.

Pied wagtails nest commonly in or near farm buildings close to ponds and streams, but yellow wagtails are only passage-migrants. Spotted flycatchers nest in all sheltered garden and semi-wooded areas, but pied flycatchers, though they have been heard singing in open woodland in the east of the county, are only recorded as scarce but regular migrants, chiefly at Skokholm. The chiffchaff is probably more abundant than the willow-warbler; it seems to breed successfully in each small isolated wood tucked into the folds of the exposed coastline, which is avoided by the willow-warbler (except on migration). Garden-warbler and blackcap have a similar relation, the blackcap nesting more freely in isolated woods of such description, and the garden-warbler seeming to prefer more sheltered, more extensively enclosed country. The goldcrest breeds but not numerously, owing to the lack of conifers in the county; it is more common and widely spread in winter. The sedge-warbler can be found singing in every overgrown water-ditch, but the reed warbler is only a rare vagrant. The lesser whitethroat appears in the spring in small numbers and calls and sings, but soon disappears again; it has only once been proved to breed.

As for the nightingale, George Owen, the historian, who was born in 1552 and died in 1613, wrote that

"there is none to be founde, nor ever anie hard in any age, whereof wee reade or heare, wch some Judge proceedeth of the coldnes of the Countrye, or for want of pleasant groves, but that is not lykely, for althoughe generallie the Countrye be champion, yet there are in the same in some partes manie sweete and pleasant groves, & valleys, And I haue heard the nightingall in Countries & places in Wales, as subiect to cold more then manie partes of Penbrokshire ys, Neither do I consent wth the fable fathered upon St. Dauids, who, as the tale goeth, being seriouse occupied in the night tyme in his divine orizons, was so troubled wth the sweete tuninges of the Nightingall, as that he cold not fasten his minde vpon heavenlie cogitacions, as at other tymes, being letted by the melodie of the bird, praied vnto th'almightie, that from that tyme forward, there might never a nightingall sing wihin his Dioces, and this saieth our weomen, was the cause of confininge of the bird out of this Countrey, thus much to recreat the readers spirittes."

But the prohibition laid (according to this fable) by St David upon the bird visiting his diocese was removed in 1948 by a nightingale which came to Pointz Castle valley, five miles from his cathedral, and sang for many nights of May. No nest was found and it appeared to be a stray bird.

Swallows and house-martins are common in Pembrokeshire, the latter frequently breeding on cliff sites around the coast. Sand-martins and swifts breed, but are not numerous except on migration.

The owls of the cultivated land are represented by the tawny owl, living in trees and in holes in wooded valley banks; the barn-owl, somewhat thinly distributed over the whole county and breeding in caves as well as buildings; and the little owl. The last species, introduced into Britain in 1874, first bred in Pembroke-shire in 1920. It became abundant quickly, but of late years it is much reduced in numbers though widely spread (except on the higher ground). When it reached the islands where the storm-petrel breeds it found this species an easy prey; there it developed the habit of killing, beheading, and storing underground, large numbers of these delightful little sea-birds. At Skokholm, the principal breeding ground of the storm-petrel, measures have to be taken each summer to remove the little owl; unfortunately there is a fresh immigration of little owls westwards to the islands each winter. During the war, from 1940 to 1946, when Skokholm Bird Observatory was closed, the little owls destroyed hundreds of these dainty birds, but today, with the owls banished, the petrels are more numerous than ever.

M. A. Mathew, first to succeed in writing and publishing a serious ornithology of Pembrokeshire (1894), suggests that were it not for the islands off the coast there would be little to write about the birds of the county. This is not exactly true, for the mainland coasts of Pembrokeshire contain almost as many breed-ing species as those of the islands, though these are not in such immense armies. But guillemots, razorbills, puffins, cormorants, shags, great and lesser black-backed, herring- and kittiwake gulls nest at various points on the high cliffs, headlands, and peninsulas from Cemaes Head in the north to St Govan's Head in the south. These cliffs are, too, the favourite retreat and nesting place of the raven, rock-pipit, chough, peregrine falcon, kestrel, buzzard and rockdove. Of these, the chough and rock-dove are of special interest and from time to time their position causes some anxiety. In many years' observation, however, from 1927 onwards, we have not observed any very appreciable change in their numbers, which must be much the same as those calculated to exist in Mathew's time. We consider that the chough is almost stationary at between thirty and thirty-six pairs. Colonel Ryves has recently shown that jackdaws have little or no influence on the well-being or otherwise of the chough, as some observers have suggested; he has also shown that in any one year there may be a number of non-breeding choughs, including paired birds, and our experience tends to confirm this (e.g. six birds frequented Skomer in the summer of 1946 but were obviously not breeding, since they remained in a compact flock from early April to October). So that the actual number of pairs breeding in Pembrokeshire each year may be well below the number of birds paired. As for the rock-dove, it is doubtful if any truly wild descendants of the original rock-dove are left, so easily does the escaped or lost homing pigeon take to a wild life and breed with its wild congeners. Observers sometimes confuse this species with the stock-dove, which also frequents and will breed in the cliffs of Pembrokeshire, though not in caverns like the rock-dove, but in holes well up on the cliff-top. The stock-dove also breeds inland in Pembrokeshire, but is not an abundant species.

Along the furze-grown tops, between the cultivated land and the cliff-face, wheatears and stonechats are common, and many pairs of meadow-pipits here touch the territory of the rock-pipits. These outer coasts, being for the most part rocky, are not suited to the habits of the majority of wading birds. The only waders which breed along the Pembrokeshire tide-line are the oyster-catcher (about 120 pairs along the whole of the mainland coast), and the ringed plover, a few pairs of which nest where there are suitable banks of shingle and sand.

It is the estuary of Milford Haven that provides the principal feeding grounds for wading birds, sea-ducks, and some of the diving birds. Of these the sheld-duck, a partial migrant, is the only summer breeder within the Haven; that is, if we except the heron which feeds commonly there and also nests in trees bordering the estuary. About twenty-five pairs of herons nest within the county, some on trees, some on sea-cliffs.

The migration of birds in Pembrokeshire is fascinating to watch. The spring migration begins as early as the middle of February when small parties of meadow-pipits appear on open heaths and fields. These birds fly as a rule steadily in a northerly direction between intervals of feeding. Their numbers increase to their maximum by the middle of March, the migration gradually ceasing during April.

A limestone stack off the Castlemartin peninsula, with guillemots nesting among the sea-mallow

Early in March there is an influx of black redstarts, a very few of which have spent the whole winter in sheltered bays and about old castle walls (e.g. Dale, Cwmyreglwys, Manorbier, Pembroke and Haverfordwest). As many as fifty of these birds have been counted in one day of March (1948) at Skokholm, and recently there appears to have been an increase in their numbers in Pembrokeshire, coincident with the increase of this species as a breeder in southern England. The movement tails off in April, although odd birds have been recorded up to June 1st.

Fieldfares, redwings, song-thrushes, blackbirds, sky-larks and starlings pass along the coast during the whole of March, in fluctuating numbers which are reduced in early April. Some fieldfares and a few redwings are recorded late in April (and sometimes in May) on the islands, but principally about the higher mountain farms of the Prescelly range, which they appear reluctant to leave in the spring.

Wheatears and chiffchaffs seldom arrive before the second week of March, and the main "rushes" appear at the end of the month, rapidly dwindling by the middle of April. In March and early April there is a strong movement of rooks, nearly all of which are wearing the black feathered "face" of the yearling bird, together with small parties of (and single) jackdaws. These birds usually appear to arrive from a south-westerly direction in north-easterly winds, suggesting a return from the direction of Cornwall or—on a wind-deflected course—from southern Ireland. None is seen on the return journey which appears to be made by some other route.

In mid- and late March chaffinches pass through, usually in large flocks flying high early in the day. A very few bramblings accompany them. These flocks move quickly and disperse rapidly; they are followed by stragglers which continue to appear well on into April. With these later arrivals are small parties of green-finches, goldfinches, linnets and pied wagtails, some of them obviously returning to breed in or near the county.

Ring-ouzels and white wagtails pass through, especially in the coastal districts, from mid-March to mid-April, to be followed by yellow wagtails from mid-April to early May.

Part of the gannetry of 10,000 nests on the uninhabited islet sanctuary of Grassholm

The first willow-warblers are trapped at Skokholm during the last week of March. This is one of the largest small bird migrations in Pembrokeshire, and for a whole month between mid-April and mid-May there are days when the county swarms with these charming singers. Whitethroats arrive in mid-April, generally in large numbers immediately, and continue on passage for a month. Cuckoos appear at the same time and pass in small numbers until mid-May.

Swallows and sand-martins rarely arrive in number before the first week of April, following stray birds which have gone ahead in March. House-martins follow in the third week of April. All these are numerous on passage, but especially the swallow, until mid-May, and wandering birds visit the islands throughout the summer. Swifts appear in the last ten days of April, continuing to fly over the islands until late in May, during which month this migration assumes a marked north-westerly trend in the direction of Ireland. Whimbrel arrive during the last few days of April, steadily flying northwards in a daily stream lasting until the end of May.

The end of April and the beginning of May bring a small army of the less abundant migrants, some of which would often be overlooked if it were not for their regular appearance in the catching-boxes of the bird traps at Skokholm. These include the pied and spotted flycatchers, the garden-, sedge, and grasshopper-warblers, blackcap, lesser whitethroat, redstart, whinchat and corn-crake. None of these species is common, and some are very scarce, on the autumn passage.

Greenland wheatears appear in some numbers at this time, too, well spread over the whole of the county, a notable migration; on the islands the larger and richer buff appearance of the cocks contrasts with the smaller size and deeper blue of the cock common wheatears, which by that time are busy with their first nests.

The last regular migrants are the nightjar, the turtle-dove and the quail, arriving in the second week in May. The nightjar quickly vanishes, but turtle-doves move leisurely, often remaining a week or more in one spot, or upon one of the islands during

May and June. Since the turtle-dove does not breed in Pembroke-shire, it is likely that these temporarily "lost" birds are individuals born in the previous year whose breeding organs are not fully developed. The quail is scarce—usually only single birds are seen.

Irregular migrants are too numerous to be dealt with in this summary; new ones are frequently recorded at Skokholm Bird Observatory. As our knowledge of west-coast migration increases we begin to realise that it is only lack of intensive obser-vation that has made some birds appear to be rare when in all probability they may be regular migrants (e.g. ortolan and Lap-land buntings and hoopoe) in Pembrokeshire.

The impulse of the spring migration is scarcely spent ere the first autumn movements begin—with the westward movement of young starlings. The starling is a scarce breeder in Pembroke-shire, and the large numbers that arrive on the coast in late June and July must come from more populous breeding areas, probably from the north and east of Wales and from England. In July too, young willow-warblers and whitethroats begin to move along the coast, becoming abundant in August; the adults follow late in that month, and all have departed by the middle of September. Much the same is true of the yellow wagtail, on a smaller scale. Young chiffchaffs and white wagtails begin to pass southwards in mid-August, and are followed much later by the adults of these two species, the last rushes of the old birds taking place during the first two weeks of October.

Water-rails are heard screaming in the bracken and waste covers of the coast and islands from mid-August onwards. There they remain common throughout the winter, the majority de-parting early in April.

Swallows and both martins begin their return migration across Pembrokeshire during the second week of September, and continue for a month, with stragglers into the first week of November. Swift migration begins in late July and is over by September 10th. The Greenland wheatear, much less numerous on the autumn passage, passes through in mid-September, in company with the young common wheatears. But some of the adult common wheatears, which are then completing their moult at the breeding grounds, remain until mid-October or even later. Adult and young cuckoos appear on the islands from mid-July to mid-August; some young cuckoos occasionally turn up in early September.

From August to October the first "winter residents" return, movements of local breeding birds mingling with those of genuine migrants from Scandinavia and Scotland. Thus curlews come down from the hills and moors of Wales and settle in large flocks along the shore, and with them are whimbrel from Arctic lands: the whimbrel pass on during September but some of the curlews remain all the winter.

Robins and wrens follow the starlings out to winter quarters on the islands; ringing has proved that the same individuals will retain a habit by returning to the same territories there each winter. It is apparently at this time of year that young dunnocks, starlings, blackbirds, stonechats and little owls settle down on the islands and, finding suitable territory, may remain to breed there —if they survive the windy conditions and the attacks of migrating hawks. In this way colonisations occur which may or may not survive many years of exposure in wind-swept isolation; for example it is interesting to note that during the war starlings began to breed at Skokholm (two pairs in 1944), where at the present time as many as forty pairs may nest; these residents appear to be entirely sedentary in that they do not join in the winter movements of, and do not cross to the mainland with starling flocks which visit the island in winter. They are thus in habit a separate race, and it is possible that, if only they survive long enough—which is very doubtful—as a unit they will, by inbreeding in isolation, begin to establish certain definable characteristics by which a "Skokholm" race of the starling will be recognised; as the Shetland Starling has done.

Mistle- and song-thrushes, greenfinches, linnets, chaffinches, sky-larks, stonechats, meadow-pipits and goldcrests, wandering from mainland homes and from hills and valleys inland in late autumn, spread over the whole of Pembrokeshire, moving little in fine open weather, but retreating westwards before frost and snow. There is also a dispersal from the coast of birds born in cliff nests. Ravens, carrion-crows and jackdaws fly inland; choughs and rock-pipits disperse along the shore and feed farther inland. As many as a hundred ravens have been counted in a flock flying inland at dusk in late autumn, presumably to some crag or mountain roosting place. The greatest number of choughs I have seen in a flock in Pembrokeshire has been sixteen.

In mid-October, usually in calm weather with light easterly breezes, one of the largest of visible migrations sets in. This is the huge movement of finches across Cardigan Bay and St George's Channel. Many thousands of chaffinches rain down upon the shores and seaward farms and woods of Pembrokeshire, arriving from out of the north-west from just before dawn until well into mid-day. It is probable that these birds have left Scottish, Irish and English shores the night before. The main bulk of this migration consists of chaffinches, but with them come bramblings, greenfinches, linnets, goldfinches, sky-larks, meadow-pipits, fieldfares, redwings, blackbirds, song-thrushes and a few starlings. It is a wonderful experience to watch this migration from a headland such as Dinas, Strumble, St David's, or one of the islands. In a few days several million birds pass over Pembrokeshire, many perhaps to settle there if the weather is inviting enough. Part of this huge army of the finches breaks up on striking the coast, and fills the stubbles and the farm yards where fallen grain and weed seeds provide abundant food. Among the arrivals the careful observer may find one or two less common species, such as snow-bunting and lesser redpoll, and we were lucky enough on one occasion to watch a pair of serins.

Of water-birds, wild swans and geese are never numerous and only remain long in hard weather. In the sheltered "pills" and inland creeks of the winding salt estuary of Milford Haven there are often large flocks of wigeon, teal, mallard, shoveler, pochard, tufted and scaup-ducks to be seen in winter; punt-gunning in the middle reaches of Milford Haven has always been popular, at least in the past. In these same waters the goldeneye, pintail, goosander and smew are frequently recorded.

The three divers—great northern, black-throated and red-throated—regularly visit the Haven, especially in rough weather when they are driven from feeding grounds at sea. Grebes, excepting the "little" species, are scarce winter visitors, chiefly inside the Haven. Herons, too, frequent the sheltered Haven in winter, but in small numbers, an early autumn migration westwards taking place over the islands.

On the considerable mud- and sand-banks exposed by the receding tide within Milford Haven rest and feed out of the breeding-season many thousands of curlew, lapwing, dunlin and redshank, with smaller parties and individuals of turnstone, knot, purple sandpiper, sanderling, greenshank and grey plover. Other waders are scarce, but lack of observers in winter in this thinly inhabited county has not contributed to a very full list. Snipe and jack snipe visit the neighbouring marshes, and woodcock haunt the rhododendron and woodland covers of the lower valleys. The common bittern is almost a regular winter visitor to these marshes and all too often is put up and shot by the sportsman out for snipe and duck.

The movements of sea-birds off the west coast of Britain recently became more comprehensible to observers with the information which intensive ringing at Skokholm and Grassholm has provided. One of the most astonishing is the daily movement of Manx shearwater and gannets from their breeding grounds in Pembrokeshire to their sardine-shoal feeding grounds southwards, even as far as the north coast of Spain. These movements have been observed off the coast of Cornwall, where the stream of southward bound birds becomes, inevitably, concentrated by the westward thrust of the Land's End; birds travelling south across the mouth of the Bristol Channel find themselves embayed (especially if drifted eastwards by the prevailing westerly winds), and forced to travel south-westwards in order to round Cornwall.

Gannet, shearwater and razorbill are all three more migratory than the guillemot. Ringing in Pembrokeshire of these species has proved that the gannet goes as far south as Senegal, the Manx shearwater (as far as ringing has proved) to the east coast of Brazil and Argentine, and the razorbill penetrates the Mediterranean as far as the French and Italian Riviera coasts. But the guillemot as a rule performs less distant migrations; where large colonies exist, as at Skomer and Ramsey and Stack Rocks (south Pembs.), the adults may visit the ledges in December, and individuals are to be seen close to the coast throughout the winter. In the breeding season razorbills do not travel far from the nesting cliff, but ringed gannets have been found up to 200 miles from Grassholm then, and the adult Manx shearwater regularly feeds in the sardine-filled waters off the north coast of Spain, leaving its mate alone on the nest brooding for two or three days while it performs this 600-mile journey! Only ringing of individuals could have proved such an interesting fact.

Puffins arrive at the island late in March; the adults depart for the open Atlantic in August, leaving the deserted young puffin (which is at first almost flightless) to make its own way to the sea, and to swim westwards into the vastness of ocean. Eventually it joins with the adults far at sea, and throughout the winter this species does not voluntarily approach the land. The little auk appears from the far north in coastal waters during mid-winter, but it is scarce, and, since the decline in winter inshore fishing by Pembrokeshire men, it is now seldom recorded, unless washed ashore dead or oiled. The migration of the cormorant has already been mentioned. The shag stays within home waters all the year, but occasionally young shags will stray as far as Ireland or Cornwall in their first winter.

Of the gulls, the lesser black-backed is the most migratory; occasionally a few, including the darker-backed Scandinavian race, are seen in winter (e.g. at Haverfordwest bridges), but the majority leave for Spain, Portugal and North Africa in September and October, and return in March. Some of the old adults arrive on the breeding islands a month earlier than the main body. The concentrations of great black-backed and herring-gulls disperse from the breeding islands during September, to take up feeding stations on mainland estuary, marsh, and field; the adults return at the first sign of spring in January and February, but will leave again during intervals of bitter weather which occur in these months. The kittiwake, settling upon its nesting cliffs in March (after spasmodic visits weeks earlier), departs again in late August and September, dispersing widely over the Atlantic; yet some of both adults and first year birds (in "tarrock" plumage) can be seen on a winter's day within sight of land. Common and black-headed gulls are abundant visitors to Pembrokeshire in winter.

In the shallow open sea around Grassholm and the Smalls and westwards of the Bishops and Clerks, during the months of August, September and October, terns, skuas, fulmar petrels, sooty, Manx and great shearwaters have been recorded by fishermen, but this promising area through lack of competent observers is almost unknown ornithologically.

Of wild flowers Pembrokeshire has a most notable collection of both inland and maritime species, including a few rare species and varieties. There is no room to list them here, but the publications of the West Wales Naturalists' Trust*may be consulted, particularly *A List of Pembrokeshire Plants* (F. L. Rees), and *The Flora of the St David's Peninsula* (C. L. Walton). But it is for the great masses of snowdrops, daffodils, primroses, cowslips and bluebells, followed by a rich succession of summer flowers, including vernal squill, sea-pink and sea-campion on the cliffs, that the county is perhaps most satisfying botanically. Urban despoilers and other rabid collectors of wild flowers have not yet reached Pembrokeshire in effective numbers, local bye-laws forbid the uprooting of plants, and we can only hope that this happy state of wild flower profusion will continue indefinitely.

* Address: 4 Victoria Place, Haverfordwest.

A SHORT BIBLIOGRAPHY

ATKINSON, R. J. C. (1956), *Stonehenge*, London.

BUXTON, John and Lockley, R. M. (1950), *Island of Skomer*, London.

DAVIES, Margaret F. (1939), *The Land of Britain* (Report of the Land Utilisation Survey of Britain, Part 32—Pembrokeshire).

EDWARDS, Emily Hewlett (1909), *Castles and Strongholds of Pembrokeshire*, Tenby.

FENTON, Richard (1903), *Historical Tour through Pembrokeshire*, Brecknock.

JONES, E. H. Stuart (195), *The Last Invasion of Britain*, London.

LAWS, Edward (1888), *The History of Little England beyond Wales*, London.

MIREHOUSE, Mary Beatrice (1910), *South Pembrokeshire*, London.

OWEN, George (1892), *Description of Pembrokeshire*, London.

OWEN, Henry (1904), *Gerald the Welshman*, London.

REES, J. F. (1954), *The Story of Milford*, Cardiff.

RICHARDS, Tom (1949), *South Wales and Monmouthshire*, London.

SMITH, Lucy Toulmin (1906), *Leland's Itinerary in Wales*, London.

West Wales Field Society, Reports and Publications, 1945–56.

WIGHT, Margaret (1954), *Pembrokeshire and the National Park*, Tenby.

also

County Development Plan, 1953 (County Council of Pembroke).

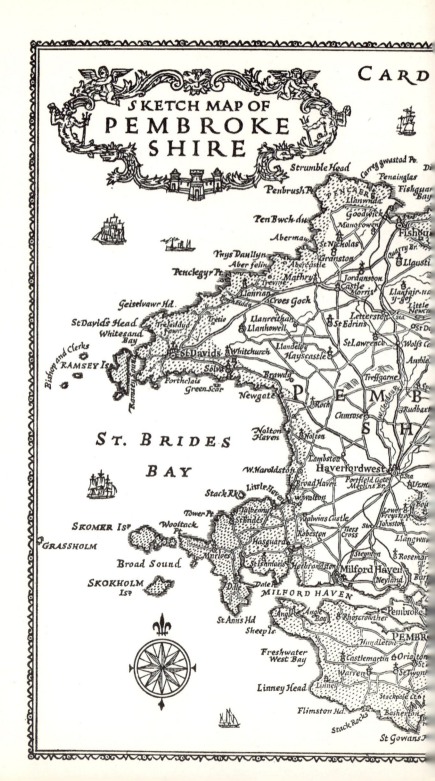

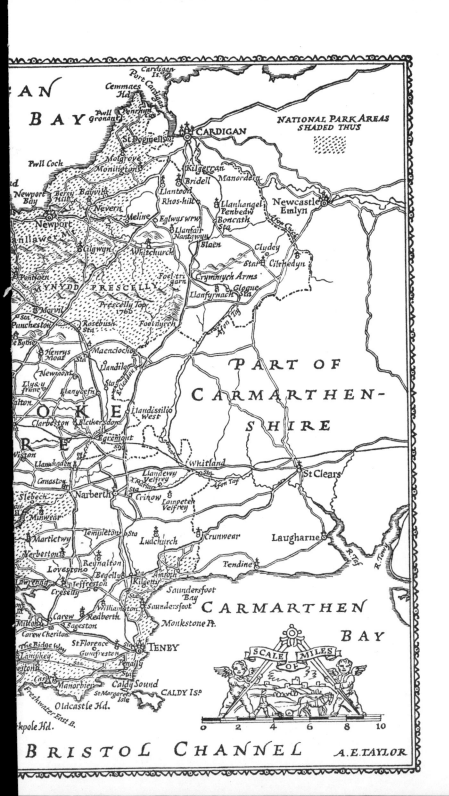

INDEX